THANK YOU FOR YOUR SUPPORT

Stephen Ysafflei

Worthy of Such Devotion

The SHAK Story

Robert MacGowan

First Edition 2018

Edited and Produced by R MacGowan

Front cover picture:
Rachel Summerson with SHAK dogs

Order this book at Amazon or any major retailer

ISBN: 978-0-244-64607-3

Shankhouse Books UK
C/o 627 Davis Drive, Morrisville, NC 27560, USA
macgowan5599@gmail.com

Acknowledgements

Thank you to Stephen Wylie for his honest memories, and for Shak.

Thanks to all the staff, volunteers, fundraisers, donators and helpers who made it all possible.

Thank you to all the veterinary staff who recognise Stephen's vision and often place their trust in him.

My thanks once again to Beverley for her support.

Photographs by Stephen Wylie, Andy Commins, Beverley MacGowan and others unknown.

Dedications

This book is dedicated to the millions of innocent animals that we torture and kill each day across the globe, for whatever reason.

Both the author and Shak generally support the RSPCA and all organisations which help animals and rescue abandoned dogs from our streets. SHAK is very much concerned with the increasing numbers which slip through the safety net for whatever reason, particularly when already in shelter.

Foreword

At 9am on Tuesday 4th July 2017 I attended a meeting with Shak founder Stephen Wylie to gather information for this book, during a break from his 24/7 work at the charity's kennels in Northumberland UK. During our discussion I asked a question about the fact that several veterinary practices ask him to take in various dogs, which have been brought to them to be terminated. He surprised me by replying, 'Oh shit,' and pulled a mobile phone from the defensively padded jeans he was wearing. 'Excuse me, won't be a minute,' he continued, poking numbers on the screen.

'No problem,' I said, taking a tentative sip of the hot black coffee I'd just bought at the Heighley Gate Garden Centre café, a mile or so along the A697 after it branches north west from the A1 towards Coldstream and the Scottish borders.

I didn't actually listen in on the ensuing conversation but it soon became clear that he was talking to a vet practice, and was definitely worried about something. After a few minutes he clicked the phone off, slid it onto the table between us and shook his head.

'Problems?' I asked, inhaling deeply to cool my tongue after burning it with the coffee.

'Yes, and I'd forgotten all about it so good job you reminded me – so much on my mind at the moment.'

'Anything I can do to help?'

'No, not really…well, actually…'

'Go on?'

'Well, I got a call a few days ago from the St Clair Vet Centre in Blyth, saying they had a three year-old Border Collie coming in to be put down, but they can't see a reason for it.'

'So they want you to take him?'

'Yes but I've already got a pick-up in Manchester this afternoon plus a thousand and one things to do tomorrow.'

'Is he at the vet's now?'

'It's a she actually and no, she was supposed to be coming in today but the vet just now managed to put the owner off until tomorrow morning. Trouble is I have to be there by nine thirty at the latest and that will mean letting somebody else down.'

'So I could pick her up?'

'You sure you can manage it and don't mind?'

'No, of course I don't mind, I'd be proud to do it.'

'You'll have to be there on time though or it might be too late.'

'I'll be there early, give me the address and postcode.'

'I'll text it to you and also for the kennels, but don't give it out generally or I'll end up with dozens of abandoned dogs tied to the gate.'

We finished our discussion and left, and I made a note about my mission for the following day. I was up early in the morning, showered but didn't bother shaving, and pulled the Shak t-shirt Stephen had given me over a black, long-sleeved cycling jersey. Along with a pair of black cargo-pants my wife said I looked like a Special Forces operative ready for action.

I arrived at the vet's early and parked nearby on Croft Road. It was around the time of the owner's arranged time for delivery of the unwanted Collie and there was an estate car parked outside, so I gave it a few minutes until a guy came out and climbed into the driver's seat. I went straight in and told the receptionist why I was there, and she said, 'Thank goodness you're here,' as she pointed to a side door.

I walked through to see a beautiful black & white Border Collie, standing nervously in the middle of three veterinary nurses.

'Oh hi,' said the one holding the dog and looking at my brand new shirt. 'This is Molly.'

'Hello Molly,' I said, bending to stroke her. 'You're beautiful.'

'Can you take her right now? We've only got about twenty minutes to go.'

'Yes, that's why I'm here. I was waiting outside for the owner to leave in case he started asking questions.'

'Well, he knows she's going to a rescue charity, but we haven't told him where so he can't land up there anytime if he realises what he's done and changes his mind.'

'Which sometimes happens,' one of the other girls added. 'Until they change their mind again and bring the poor animal back to us.'

'Did he say what the problem was?'

'Ha, you won't believe this: at the same time he booked her in for euthanasia he also booked first vaccinations for a new puppy!'

'What! You're joking?'

'Afraid not, just like he was trading in a used car! He said he and his wife had split up so he only saw the kids at weekends now, and Molly's supposed to have snapped at one of them. They told their mother and she said he couldn't have the kids to visit unless he got rid of the dog!'

'And he just did as he was told?'

'Yes and I suppose that might be just about understandable at a push – apart from the fact that he went straight out and bought a replacement!'

'Well it's a good thing you didn't tell him where she's going – because he won't be getting to see her again no matter how many times he changes his mind.'

'And if he did manage to get Molly back, guess what would happen to the new pup?'

'Oh Christ, couldn't you have tripped over and stuck the needle in him instead, accidentally of course?'

We all laughed and I left, opened the back of the Range Rover and Molly jumped straight in. She had a sniff around at the scents left there by my own German Pointer, Oscar, then settled down without a problem

Up at the Shak kennels she leapt out when asked to and I kept her on the leash whilst talking to Stephen and the other staff.

At one point a loud metallic bang rang out as one of the kennel gates clanged shut, and Molly moved closer to me, pressing against my leg for reassurance in the strange environment. I reached down to pat her on the head and she looked up at me with big brown, sorrowful eyes and my heart went out to her. Stephen took her into the kennels and bedded her down as well as possible amid the chorus of barking from the other dogs at a newcomer, but later told me she settled in well and never complained, bless her.

He carried out a series of behavioural tests on her which revealed no major issues, and a few weeks later she was re-homed with a very active local couple who give her all the exercise she needs. Molly has a wonderful life now, is loved and cared for and mixes freely with children of different ages, all of whom are horrified that she was almost put to death for no reason.

Rob MacGowan 2018

Oscar

Chapter One

TROY

og 43 was picked up wandering the streets of Ashington, Northumberland, abandoned and starving on a cold, rainy night. He was a white American Bulldog with brindle patches over his right eye and haunches, and bore the scars both mentally and physically of previous long term abuse. Although malnourished he remained muscular, weighing around 35kg, and was quite a handsome dog. He was 2 to 3 years old but none of his history was known, no enquiries from the public or previous owners were made about him and because of his breed and unpredictable temperament, he was listed for euthanasia.

'Such a shame,' said Carol, one of the shelter workers, unwrapping a chocolate bar as she peered into Dog 43's cage.

'What is?' asked her colleague Alec, watching the confection as she bit it in half.

'This one,' she answered, nodding at the cage.

'Oh right - not our problem.'

'He's a good-looking boy though and seems pretty quiet most of the time - such a shame to put him to sleep so soon.'

'He'll not be the only one this time around, some of the Staffies have been with us over a month now and we're way overcrowded.'

'Yeah, the bulldog's only been here a week though.'

'What's the difference?' asked Alec, pulling out his crumpled newspaper to end the conversation. 'One week, four weeks, what's it matter?'

'Mm, what was the name of that place in the Chronicle last week?'

'What place?'

'The no-kill shelter.'

'Oh, yeah…can't remember now.'

Alec shook the paper to straighten it out and adjusted his glasses. Carol slid the other half of the chocolate bar into her mouth and looked at him, chewing slowly without blinking.

'Oh alright,' he gave in after a few silent seconds, pulling his mobile phone from a breast pocket and pushing its buttons.

Carol smiled.

'Liz,' he shouted at the phone. 'Can you check last week's Chronicle online and get me a number for that dog-shelter up country somewhere?'

He clicked off and they both sat silently for a few minutes, making the most of the rest of their break before the phone beeped back into life, playing the Rocky theme tune.

'Hello,' he answered. 'What? Yeah, that's the one, cheers Liz, see you later.'

He slipped the phone back into his pocket as Carol swallowed the last of her chocolate and asked, 'Well?'

'Shack, it's called the Shack. Sounds more like a fancy pub in the toon.'

'Yes, that's it.'

'It's up near Alnwick though. I doubt they'll come all the way down here for one stray mutt.'

'Think we could run him up there?'

'No way, we'd end up getting sacked.'

'Well did you get a phone number?'

'Liz is texting it in a minute,' he answered as his mobile beeped.

He dragged it out again, clicked the screen on and turned it towards his workmate. She held her own, bright pink phone up and recorded the displayed number into it.

'Right,' he said, re-folding his unread newspaper. 'Let's get back to work.'

'I'll just make the call and see what happens - nothing to lose, right?'

One hour later a dusty white van pulled up outside the shelter, Dog 43 was led out on two rigid leads by Carol and Alec, and hoisted up into the van which then sped north again.

At the Shak sanctuary it was soon discovered that the chunky stray wasn't at all socialised to either people or other dogs, and when the communal barking was at its loudest, Dog 43 began spinning and yelping, and lunging at the partitions of his pen, trying to get at whatever was on the other side.

'How many spare pens have we got right now?' asked Stephen, Shak's founder.

'Just two at the moment but I don't know for how long - we're getting calls from all over the place,' answered his girlfriend, Rachel.

'I know but for now let's clear the pen either side so he can't hear anything - it's obviously upsetting him.'

They did so with the help of two volunteers, but it didn't take long to see that it hadn't made any difference. Dog 43 kept on fence-chasing and failing to respond positively to human or canine presence.

'There's something different about this one,' Stephen said, scratching his close-cropped head. 'Something about the way he looks at me that I've never seen before.'

'Do you think we can reach out to him?' asked Rachel.

'I'm hoping so but it might take a bit longer than usual.'

'Well let's start by giving him a name so we know who we're talking about, any suggestions?'

'It's going to take something special to get through the defences he's built up around him, something a bit different maybe. What was the name of that wooden horse in the olden days?'

'You mean the wooden horse of Troy?'

'Yeah that's it, let's call him Troy?'

'Troy - the wooden horse dog?'

Stephen nodded with a smile.

'Okay, that kinda fits.'

Troy continued to be very unhappy when confined inside the sanctuary, but transformed into a different animal when taken outside in the fresh air and wide open spaces, both of which are more than plentiful in Northumberland, the ancient home of English civilisation. He remained a long way from being declared civilised or even safe though, so wasn't allowed unsupervised contact with any staff members except Stephen, who began socialisation by taking him for short walks on-lead around the sanctuary perimeter.

Once outside Troy relaxed immediately and Stephen guessed he'd never been walked regularly before, but probably kept locked up inside a pen possibly as a guard-dog, or even trained to be aggressive by some street-thug who used him as a status symbol of the strength he lacked himself. Understandably, Troy became agitated at being penned up again and resumed defensive behaviour immediately.

As summer approached and the Northumbrian weather improved slightly prior to the early May holiday weekend, Stephen and Troy set off on a longer trek into the Cheviot foothills. They'd known each other for three months now and were a lot more at ease in close contact. Stephen had been looking forward to this day and once far enough out into the vast landscape, he let the dog off-leash for the first time.

It immediately ran around in circles, enjoying the space and freedom, and being alive. They carried on walking, still ascending until coming to a wide, metal gate approached by a cattle-grid with 2-inch spaces between the bars. Troy was ahead but stopped to wait for Stephen to catch up, gently lift and slowly carry him across the grid. Troy kept perfectly still until back on his feet, then ran off up the hill with his stumpy tail wagging like an excited puppy.

At the brow Stephen sat on the grass, gazing around at the panoramic views stretching for hundreds of miles in all directions, and Troy sat with him, panting hard to cool down. Stephen lay back, looking up at white clouds banking in from the West, and Troy lay right next to him, closing his eyes and laying his massive head on Stephen's chest.

They basked in the sun for an hour; Troy snoring and Stephen pondering how he could ensure a relaxed, positive atmosphere in which the troubled dog could continue to recover from his past traumas. Could he be fostered out? - certainly not yet. Could Stephen take him home to continue therapy 24/7? - no because there were already eight dogs resident in continuing treatment after release from the sanctuary. Could anything be changed at the sanctuary itself to provide ideal conditions? - he'd have to consider that one in detail but in the meantime, there was no option available other than to keep him there for now. They'd definitely built up some trust between them but could he leave the dog alone with anybody else, including trained staff? - again no, at least not yet because in the event of one small mistake, Troy was powerful enough to inflict very serious injury.

They returned to the sanctuary refreshed but on approaching the pens, Troy pulled away. He didn't want to go back inside but with no other choice, Stephen pushed him in and closed the gate. Troy froze where he stood, a yard inside the pen, and slowly turned to look back at his jailer with an ice-cold stare. Stephen looked back at the big dog, slightly concerned about the expression on its face, and after the pleasant day they'd just spent together – he couldn't escape the feeling that locking him up again was an act of betrayal.

Two

ATTACK

The main sanctuary building is a big, rectangular ex cattle shed with an entrance at one end. Inside, the pens are arranged in a u-shape around the other three walls, separated by metal partitions which are solid for the lower section, with bars above extending to eight feet high. The central area is sectioned into runs, which contain the animals when their pens are being cleaned, and to one side of this area is an ex-storage container converted to a ball-pool for the recovering dogs to play in. The balls are actually discarded plastic bottles but the dogs don't mind in the slightest as they bounce around for hours, crunching them to recycled destruction.

The day after their Cheviots walk, Stephen entered the kennels to take Troy out again. All the staff were busy cleaning and the bulldog had been safely transferred to the adjacent run by simply opening the connecting door of his pen, and letting him walk through. Stephen opened the gate to see him fence-chasing again, stopping periodically to sniff at the partitions when he sensed a presence on the other side. He couldn't see anything but could smell and hear clearly, which aroused his defences and told of the torture he'd previously experienced.

As Stephen stepped inside the cage, Troy stopped dead in his tracks and without looking up, walked slowly to the farthest corner and sat down to stare at the wall beyond the bars. Stephen was puzzled but remembering how happy they'd been just the day before, called to him, 'Come on Troy, we're going out in the hills again.'

The big dog ignored him.

'Come on boy, let's go.'

There was still no response so Stephen took a few wary steps towards him, stopping six feet away. He knew by the dog's body language that something was wrong, and as Troy turned slowly to look at him, a chill of fear ran down his spine. The dog stared at him with a glazed expression, black eyes blank and emotionless, and Stephen knew he had to get out of there fast. Before moving he turned his head to the side, avoiding eye contact and confrontation. This appeasement though to a dog not used to it, was probably interpreted as simple weakness and Troy now turned to face the human who'd betrayed him.

Stephen backed off a few paces, raised his palms towards the dog in a calming gesture and said softly, 'Okay Troy, no rush - take your time.'

The dog tensed, muscles bunched and eyes fixed on Stephen, who now knew he was in grave danger. He was about to run when Troy let out a short, low-pitched growl and launched himself forward like an uncoiling spring.

It was thought that the fighting-breed dog had been trained to be viciously aggressive and is possible that when Stephen raised his hands as a peace gesture, it was reminded of being repeatedly beaten as part of that training. Whatever the cause it must have been major and disastrous, because it clamped its powerful jaws around Stephen's left bicep and pulled him easily to the ground. The back of Stephen's head hit the hard-packed earth and he lay dazed, with the bulldog's teeth mere inches from his face.

He'd been bitten by other breeds, numerous times and all were slightly different, but Troy was something else – he was more like a shark as he shifted his jaws to get a better, deeper hold. The dog was concentrating on his arm, the one that had held the lead, but Stephen knew that with one swift turn of the head it could be his throat, and probable death.

Suddenly he heard a scream and fearing that Rachel would enter the arena, he ignored the searing pain and jerked himself into a sitting position. Troy kept his grip but Stephen forced him backwards and struggled to his knees, and then his feet, keeping his right arm between the dog's now-bloody teeth and his neck. Then the gate opened and as the two volunteers shouted at the rampant animal, trying to distract it, Rachel rushed in wielding a sweeping brush.

'Get out Rachel,' Stephen shouted. 'He's totally lost control.'

She continued forward, holding the broom in front of her like a spear.

'Rachel,' Stephen screamed in panic. 'Get out of here now and stay out.'

10

'You need help,' she cried back, tears running down her face.

'I can handle this now,' he answered, shock dissipating and determination returning as he jammed two fingers into Troy's nostrils to stop him breathing.

He hoped the dog would have to release his arm to breathe through his mouth but the technique didn't work, and Troy pushed his quarry back against the fence with a deep growl.

Stephen forced himself to keep calm and wrestled with the dog in an attempt to stay on his feet, as going down again now could be fatal. Rachel backed off and he could hear her crying from the gateway, but at least she was outside and safe.

The dog was becoming more agitated as they engaged in a death-dance around the cage, and it wrenched its head from side to side in an effort to pull him off his feet. He had to loosen its grip on him if he was to escape, and shoved his fingers back into the animal's nostrils from behind to jerk its head backwards. It released its hold, turned immediately and sank its teeth into Stephen's right arm. He pulled it off again and the dog went for his leg, so he grabbed the collar with both hands and heaved upwards, but the dog resisted fiercely. He almost toppled at that point but grasped the collar again, pulling and twisting with all his remaining strength in a last ditch effort, and the dog showed the first sign of giving up the fight as its emotions returned to something like normal.

'Open the gate now,' Stephen croaked.

The gate opened and he dragged Troy towards it, pushing him backwards at the last moment and stumbling out as it clanged shut again. He fell to the floor exhausted, chest heaving, trousers and shirt ripped to ribbons, and blood pouring from several wounds to both arms and legs.

'Oh no,' gasped Rachel, visibly distraught as she helped him up and into the cabin. 'You have to go to hospital right now.'

'I'll be fine,' he protested as volunteer Laura assessed his gaping wounds.

'No you won't,' she said.

'No, you won't,' Rachel agreed. 'And we've already called an ambulance anyway.'

'You could drive me there.'

'No, you need urgent attention – you're lucky to be alive.'

'Well if I'm going to hospital I need to make sure Troy's secure – what if that was one of you in there instead of me?'

'One of us would be dead by now – that's what. Now shut up and save your strength until the ambulance gets here.'

He was stretchered aboard and rushed to Wansbeck General A&E at Ashington, with blue lights flashing and siren wailing, and given gas & air plus a morphine injection en-route. He was trolleyed straight into triage, x-rayed and physically checked to record all damage, then cleaned, sterilised, bandaged up and transferred to the intensive care unit.

He'd been whisked away to hospital before Rachel could clamber into the ambulance with him, so to allay her mounting panic she telephoned Joan and told her what had happened.

'Right, I'm off to the hospital,' she replied. 'Where's the dog now?'

'It's still in the pen but the gate's not very secure and he still seems a bit crazy.'

'Definitely do not go in there - call the er, call a vet right away for advice.'

Rachel rang the closest practice and asked for urgent assistance, but a newly qualified young woman turned up and refused to go anywhere near the drooling dog, which was now spinning in circles as it growled and lunged at the bars.

'I'm going to call out an armed police officer to deal with this animal before it injures anybody else,' the vet declared.

That didn't seem right to Rachel so she called Joan again, who by then was at Stephen's hospital bedside.

'An armed police officer?' she asked in surprise.

Stephen heard his mother's response to the call and grabbed the phone from her. 'No way is he going to be shot in the back of the head like Kyle,' he shouted as loudly as he could manage. 'Please don't let that happen to him, Rachel.'

She immediately rang the vet's office and asked for a more experienced member of staff to attend, and was assured that one was on the way.

Stephen was additionally diagnosed with severe shock which prevented corrective surgery at that point, placed under 24-hour observation and admitted to theatre the following day for repairs to the bone-deep gashes in his body.

All dogs' teeth carry a heavy payload of bacteria and although bleeding might reduce the threat of calamitous infection, it remained severe and Stephen was still in hospital three days later.

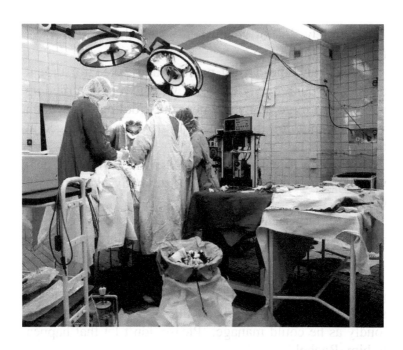

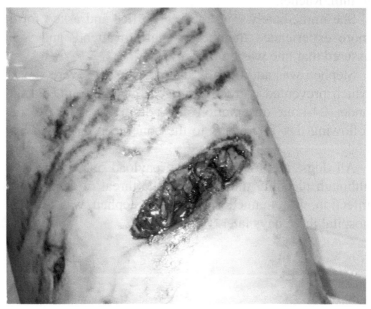

Three

FOUNDATIONS

Stephen Wylie was born at Newcastle-upon-Tyne in 1974 but his father, Ian, was a civil-servant and at two years old, the toddler was moved to London along with his mother Joan and six year-old sister, Karen.

Stephen can't recall much about this time obviously, but does remember that one afternoon his parents came home with a little, four-legged ball of fluff which immediately stole everybody's hearts, and after a quick poll was named Prince. The dog was a Rough Collie and a dead-ringer for film star, Lassie, who the whole family loved watching on television. He soon became little Stephen's constant companion.

When pressure from work eased up on Ian, he moved the family back to the North East where life was more relaxed, and took up residence in a new house at Hadrian Park, a few miles east of Newcastle at Wallsend. This is where the Roman Wall built by Hadrian and stretching from the Solway Firth in the west, terminates in the east on the north bank of the River Tyne.

Life wasn't simple for the young boy though, fitting back into a north-east school with a slightly southern accent, but Prince never judged him and was always waiting excitedly with a wagging tail for his return.

Stephen's other two loves were football and motor cars, and when rain stopped play on the pitch he'd lay on the sheepskin rug at home, in front of the fire, steering his *matchbox* motors up and down the mountain that was

Prince, who kept perfectly still as miniature Jaguars were parked on his head, Land Rovers trundled through the forest of his fluffy tail, and slower marques sometimes received an encouraging nudge from his cold, damp nose.

Stephen was a keen footballer but in Newcastle, competition at all levels was fierce. He loved the game though and persevered, and learned early in life about putting in the required effort. He was a grafter on the pitch who wasn't often caught in the limelight, but always got the job done. His efforts and reliability allowed him to play regularly for local teams as he grew up, often as captain, and he fell naturally into the position of fullback - already a defender, and protecting those creatures which couldn't do it for themselves was to become a major driving force in his life.

One night when Stephen was lying in bed thinking about the next day at Middle School, he heard a sound which caused him to sit up and switch the bedside lamp on - Prince was crying. He got up quietly so as not to disturb anyone else, and crept downstairs. The dog hadn't been well for a few days and was lying on his bed whimpering. He looked at Stephen as the boy lay down beside him, and placed a paw on his shoulder. Stephen stayed with him most of the night, wondering whether to wake his parents but eventually Prince calmed down, seemed more comfortable, and he went back to bed.

In the morning poor Prince was dead. He'd simply died of old age after a good life, but his passing had a serious impact on the young boy. He loved the dog, which loved him in return and he experienced great loss. Love does not differentiate between people and animals – the effects are exactly the same and Stephen would never forget the pain caused by the death of his best friend.

He was the last person to see Prince alive, and wished more than anything that he'd stayed with him - right to the end. He wished he'd remained with his dog and made its passing as easy as possible, and that feeling of helping those creatures that need it because they rely on us so much - stayed with him.

The family often visited Joan's cousin - Aunty Lillian from Crook, northwest of Bishop Auckland in County Durham. Stephen loved to visit Lillian because she had a passion for rescuing dogs, and had no less than fifteen Japanese Chins around the house plus two German Shepherds. He found the atmosphere exciting and was fascinated by the Chins which he thought looked like Papillons, whose French names referred to their erect ears resembling the wings of a butterfly.

What really struck and spellbound him though, were the two big Shepherds. Initially they reminded him of Prince, being of similar size and colour, but as he got to know them he admired their physical strength and power, their intelligence and the fact that many were used as Police, Army and other services' dogs. He knew that Shepherds regularly put their lives at risk to help people, and many are killed or injured in the line of duty. Although the visits waned as Stephen became a young man in the 1990s and gained new interests, he never forgot Aunty Lillian and her dogs.

Most young boys are easily impressed, often by people or events which lead them down certain paths, and Stephen was certainly learning some important lessons about the everyday realities of life. At the age of twelve he suffered a life-changing shock when, following differences between his parents, his mother decided that leaving was the best option for all concerned. Obviously she had her reasons, was soon divorced and the children stayed with Ian, though both remained in close contact with their mother. Despite this serious disruption the lad showed true grit, buckled down to pass all his exams and take a healthy record with him to Monkseaton High School, near the house they moved into after parental separation.

He enjoyed life at West Monkseaton (derived from: West Monks' Sea Town) in Whitley Bay, continued to do well at school and passed A-Levels in Business Studies and English. He loved living near the coast; regularly visited the beach with his new neighbours or school friends, and life seemed to be going relatively well for him. Ian got married again to a very nice lady called Sue, and they also acquired three cats.

One of his new interests was those strange, bewitching creatures - girls and at the age of seventeen, one in particular. His girlfriend Karen was a music student about to continue her studies at Nene College, in Northampton town centre. Stephen was enjoying the luxury of being a sixth-form student though actually studying anything was the last thing on his mind. He had far more important interests and was busy protesting publicly with like-minded friends, who challenged society's attitudes to such atrocities as unregulated slaughterhouses, the fur-trade and vivisection. He was a fan of sympathetic musicians such as The Smiths and Morrissey, who wrote the song which became an anthem for people who rightly believe that murdering or maiming animals for any reason is horrific and unforgivable: 'Meat is Murder'.

Stephen became a vegetarian at the age of fifteen when, eating steak & chips at his father's birthday party in a pub at Forest Hall, he noticed how much meat was left on people's plates to be thrown in the bin. He thought about the torture that millions of innocent, intelligent and deeply feeling animals have to suffer to keep people over-fed; how they're transported great distances without food, water or rest to be bludgeoned or have their throats hacked before being hung upside-down, often still kicking, on conveyor hooks for transportation to our tables. He put down his fork and quietly mentioned his revulsion to a friend who asked, 'So why aren't you a vegetarian?'

'I...I'm thinking about it,' he replied, feeling like a failure.

'Go on then, what're you waiting for?'

'I...er...alright then, I will.'

'Yeah right, when exactly?'

'Now, right now,' he answered, pushing his plate away. 'I'm now a vegetarian!'

'Ha, you'll never keep it up.'

'Oh yes I will.'

And he did.

At almost eighteen years old with no general plans or direction in place, Stephen enrolled at Nene College with Karen in 1991, to study Computing & Business Studies, both of which linked up with his A-Level qualifications. He played at being a student and hung out with Karen for a while, but soon got bored and when he met up with two old friends from Newcastle for a beer at Christmas, he noticed that Alan and Gareth were both flush with ready cash.

'You two seem to be doing alright,' he said with a little envy. 'How're the jobs going?'

'We're doing fine so thank you for putting a word in for us with your dad,' answered Alan.

'No problem, so what do you actually do?'

'Oh, it's mostly confidential stuff, down at the government offices at Manors.'

'Right,' said Stephen, noticing their expensive clothes in comparison to his jeans and tee-shirt. 'Well I'm glad you're both doing so well - must be your round at the bar is it?'

He decided there and then that he wasn't going back to college, but didn't relish the thought of working nine to five in an office either after enduring years in stuffy classrooms. He scanned the local employment ads, took a monotonous job preparing lithographs for a printing company and was bored to distraction within three months, but stayed for three years. Eventually, during one of many nights out around the holiday town of Whitley Bay, he bumped into another old school buddy who was working as an in-store salesman at the Silverlink, North Shields branch of retailer, Comet.

'Oh yeah, what's that like then?' Stephen asked, swigging a cold lager.

'It's a job, y'know – five days plus most weekends.'

'What's the money like?'

'Not bad, all things considered. There's a basic which isn't brilliant but we can bump it up quite a bit with commission.'

'Right, commission, how's that work then?'

'Basically, the more you sell - the more you get. It's not unusual for the best salesmen to double their wage.'

'Wow, really?'

'Yeah, no problem.'

'And it's face-to-face selling is it, not over the phone?'

'Yeah, you'll have met dozens of us in different shops. Anyway, why you asking all this - you looking for a change?'

'Mm, maybe but I'm not sure I'd be any good at selling stuff.'

'Yeah, you would, you got the smile and the patter. Want me to have a word with my boss?'

Stephen attended for interview a week later, was offered a job and immediately found that he did indeed have a flair for selling. After a few months learning the systems he was switched between branches to strengthen the teams during heavy footfall periods, moving from Silverlink to Gateshead and as far south as Stockton or Hartlepool. He made decent money and enjoyed the work, until sales staff were put under increased, unrelenting pressure to increase income to the company. Part of this strategy was the introduction of 'add-ons' including prolonged warranties, service contracts and extended insurance. This over-mercenary approach disillusioned Stephen and eventually, completely spoiled the job for him. He decided to leave and responded to an advertisement for sales staff at the Sony Centre in Eldon Gardens - part of the big Eldon Square complex in Newcastle city centre, and also over the famous Tyne Bridge at the colossal Metro Centre outside Gateshead. Again he was offered a position immediately, working between the two sites and settled into what was for him, a more rewarding structure.

Four

INDEPENDENCE

By his early twenties in 2002 Stephen had achieved quite a settled, productive life with plenty of friends and was still living at home with his father, stepmother, stepsister Joni and the three cats. Sister Karen had her own flat at Shiremoor with Badger, her rescued Border Collie cross. Just in from work one evening after selling increasing numbers of a recent invention: the mobile telephone, he got a call from her on his preferred model.

'Hello,' he answered, disentangling the plastic aerial from his striped silk tie.

'Hey Steve, how are you?'

'Fine sis, how's yourself?'

'Good, I'm good. I was just wondering if you had anything planned for the week after next?'

'Er, nothing important I don't think, why?'

'I'm going on holiday and wondered whether you'd look after Badger and the flat for a week?'

'Any food thrown in?'

'Of course, the fridge'll be full and I'll stash a few beers in there as well.'

'It's a deal,' he laughed.

He moved in on Sunday afternoon and as soon as Karen left the following morning, found that he liked being in control of the space around him, even temporarily. He flopped onto the sofa with a beer and his feet up to watch World Cup matches from South Korea, ate what he wanted when he felt like it, and came back after a night out at whatever time it happened to be. I could definitely get used to this lifestyle, he thought, and either buying or renting a home of his own stuck in his mind.

'How did it go, then?' Karen asked when she returned with a light suntan and heavy suitcase full of duty-free goods. 'Was Badge okay?'

'It went really well as it happens Karen, and me and Badger were just fine.'

'Oh good. No problems with the flat?'

'No, no problems at all, in fact I've decided to rent a place myself.'

'Rent one? Why the hell would you do that?'

'I like the idea of having my own place.'

'Yeah, I get that but don't rent - buy!'

'Well yeah, I know what you're saying but I'm not sure I'd qualify for a mortgage.'

'I don't see why not - you've got a steady job and good credit I presume, so just start off with something small that you can afford, like I did.'

'Like a flat?'

'Yes, like a flat, in fact…'

'What?'

'In fact you could buy this flat if you like it so much!'

'This flat? Your flat?'

'Yes, I've been thinking about moving up the ladder for a while now.'

They looked into the details, Stephen applied for a mortgage, was successful and the purchase process was set in motion. The procedure rolled along smoothly until the mortgage lender instructed an official valuation, which uncovered a problem with the communal roof and who exactly was responsible for its maintenance. The legal complications caused Stephen's mortgage application to be rejected for that particular property, until further clarification but that proved to be impossible within an acceptable timescale. Stephen remained determined to buy a property though, so scoured the local area and finally found a one-bed starter-home back at Hadrian Park. He bought it just in time as his father, assuming Stephen was moving into Karen's flat, sold up and downsized.

Shortly after the triumphal excitement of buying a house, Stephen inevitably came face-to-face with the costs and responsibilities of running it. Demands for his hard-earned money came cascading through the letter-box and changed his lifestyle instantly, curtailing his social life drastically but he reassessed and reorganised to cope.

He worked until 8pm most nights to earn extra money, refrained from going out at weekends, switched lights off when they weren't needed, never left taps running and never filled the kettle more than halfway. Surviving financially was a struggle on his own but he knew all the sacrifices would be worth it in the long haul, and looked for alternatives to allay the boredom that encroached because of them. He felt empowered and enriched by home ownership, but knew that hanging onto it would be a continuous battle.

One early sacrifice he made was his treasured 1984 BMW Convertible, which he sold for cash and replaced with a Nissan Micra bought for £120! 'If I get three months out of it without a breakdown I'll be happy,' he told himself. 'And at least it's got a digital clock which the BM didn't!'

Lying on his second-hand sofa one night, watching TV and thinking how miserable life had become, he thought back to his week at Karen's flat in Shiremoor, which had originally steered him down the path to his present predicament. He considered how deceptive his stay had been, not being responsible for any costs or expenses, and about how he'd spent that luxurious week. Suddenly he sat up with a start, eyes staring straight ahead into belated comprehension as his brick-sized phone slid to the floor. 'That's it!' he declared out loud. 'I wasn't there alone at all - I had Badger with me!'

The penny dropped with a resounding clatter into a perfectly-fitting slot; a dark cloud shifted and the light of joyful realisation shone through: 'I can get a dog of my own now without anybody else's permission!'

He'd always wanted to do so but never had the opportunity because somebody else - specifically his parents, had always been in charge of his life and the environment in which he lived it. Now though, he was free to please himself. Dogs weren't cheap to look after properly, he knew that, but what a fantastic investment in his present and future happiness!

Life immediately looked better. He was brighter and more efficient at work and in quiet moments, couldn't help smiling at the adventure he was about to embark upon. On Sunday afternoon he drove over in the Nissan to Weston Vale animal shelter, on the outskirts of the city.

The shelter takes in abandoned and unwanted cats, dogs, small furry animals and even donkeys on occasion. Stephen knew that re-homing a rescued dog is far more responsible than buying one, and thereby fuelling the breeding trade which adds to the thousands of discarded strays. He also knew that crossbreeds are usually healthier in essential structure, than those bred with various whims and fashions and sales-potential in mind.

He avoided Reception, still unsure of what he actually wanted and unwilling to discuss possibilities at that point. He needed to see the animals first so branched left and entered the main block, where he was amazed and saddened by the number of lost, homeless dogs locked up in just one shelter. He saw in every pair of eyes that followed him, the desperate longing to be with a person - a good person who would care and return the love every dog can give in abundance.

Partway along the left-hand row of metal cages, one was draped with a sheet and displayed a sign written in felt-pen saying: Unavailable for Rehoming. He checked that nobody was watching before nipping around to the back of the cage, from where he could see a frightened little terrier. He guessed that the dog couldn't be re-homed because it had behavioural problems arising from previous ill-treatment, but what he didn't realise at that time was that those treatable problems had condemned the confused little animal to death.

Stephen was interested in seeing all the dogs so made his way along the row to the end, looking in each cage to see the same, desperately-pleading expression in every one, and then crossed to the opposite row of pens. In the first one, right on the corner, he saw something different.

A small, scraggy looking ball of black & tan-coloured fluff lay despondently in the corner, but as Stephen moved into view it exploded into a four-legged frenzy which charged straight across to him. He knelt to put the back of his hand to the bars, and the puppy first sniffed before licking his fingers.

'Hello little fella,' he said, and the dog's tail wagged so fast it became a blur.

It looked about six months old and had strong German Shepherd genetics, though probably not a pedigree. A group of visitors came along and stopped by the cage as one of them said, 'Oh look, a puppy.'

The pup was distracted by the additional attention but Stephen kept watching it, and every few seconds it turned to look back at him, as if checking he was still there. The others moved along and the dog came back to Stephen, pushing its nose through the bars and wagging its tail wildly when he stroked it. He spoke again, softly and then it did something strange - it trotted back to its bed, grabbed the tattered blanket in its teeth and started shaking it. Stephen watched, intrigued until it finally chewed a piece off, brought it over and passed it through the bars to him. He was amazed and took it, realising that this little homeless puppy had given him some of the only thing in the world that it could, apart from its friendship. It brought a lump to his throat and he reached through the bars to stroke the little animal again, before standing and moving back, unwilling to engage further.

The puppy emitted a little whimper and sat on its haunches, looking at Stephen with confused disappointment. He walked slowly along the remaining pens, peering into each one until he came to the end, when he glanced back towards the pup, still sitting silently in the same position; watching him forlornly until he disappeared through the door.

He strode across the yard, feeling the first drops of a rain-shower and thinking about all the dogs he'd seen, including the nervous terrier which obviously needed help. He stopped at the public footpath, gazing out across busy Weston Road before turning left towards the rear yard where his trusty Micra was parked. Then he turned left again, back into the official entrance and Reception.

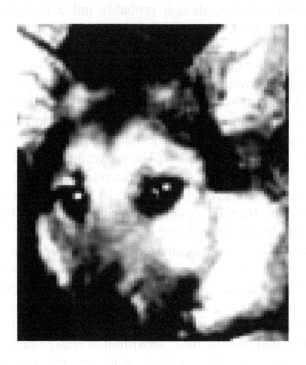

Five

THE FIRST

'Hello,' said a young girl from behind a chest-high counter, ballpoint poised over an A4 ledger.

'Hello,' replied Stephen. 'Er, the end cage on the right-hand side?'

'This end or the far end?'

'The…er…the far end.'

'Right,' she said, leafing through the ledger.

Stephen followed her gaze as if she might show him a photograph.

'Oh right,' she repeated. 'The German Shepherd cross puppy?'

'Yes that's the one. Can I take him for a little walk?'

'Oh, yes, just a minute and I'll get somebody to bring him through,' she replied, picking up her phone.

He took hold of the leash and walked the pup through the entrance area and around to the yard where his car was parked. The young man that brought the dog through watched him from the corner. The pup trotted along happily, sniffing the ground here and there but not pulling too hard, and occasionally glancing up at Stephen with a wagging tail. As he walked back into Reception the girl smiled and asked, 'What do you think of him?'

'I think he's great, can I take him home?'

'Oh, er yes I would think so, do you mean right now?'

'Yes can I take him right now?'

'Well we have some paperwork to complete first so I'll just put him back in his cage while we go through it.'

'No, don't put him back in there, where do I sign?'

Stephen kept him on the leash as they went through the documentation, until they got to the end.

'Right,' the girl said again. 'That's all done now and no problems, so there's just the fee.'

'The fee?'

'Yes, we charge a fee for his checks, vaccinations, microchip and paperwork, and to make sure people take animal adoption seriously, you know?'

'Okay, I understand, so how much is it?'

'For a dog it's a hundred pounds, please.'

'A hundred pounds?' Stephen repeated, patting his pockets.

'Yes please.'

'Well look, I haven't got a hundred on me. Can you keep hold of him while I whiz up to the bank? It's not far away.'

'Er, yes that's not a problem,' she replied with a half smile, glancing out the window at his battered car and obviously thinking the would-be adopter had changed his mind because of the fee. 'I'll have to put him back in his cage though,' she added, taking hold of the leash as if Stephen might whisk the dog off without paying.

'Okay,' he said, handing him over. 'Don't worry little pup,' he added as the dog gazed up at him. 'I'll be back before you know it.'

And he was, with the required funds which he handed over before taking the pup out again and placing him on the back seat of the car. From there he drove to the nearest supermarket, with the pup's head resting on his shoulder to buy food, bowls, a collar and lead, and as he returned to the Micra in the big car park, he bumped into his mother.

'Hello son,' she said with a beaming smile. 'What are you doing over here?'

'There's someone I'd like you to meet, mam.'

'Really?' she asked, glancing at the car, expecting his latest girlfriend to pop out.

'Haven't named him yet though,' Stephen said, opening the car door.

'Oh, oh he's beautiful,' exclaimed Joan, seeing the new puppy for the first time.

'He's still a bit straggly yet but he will be beautiful when I've sorted him out.'

Stephen checked his prized digital clock when he got back in the car with the shopping - it was 14.23 on the 7th March 1999 – only ten months before the start of the new millennium, and he knew something good had just started in his life.

Back at Hadrian Park the pup was given the run of the house and galloped around exploring its new home, but returned every few minutes to check that Stephen was still sitting in the lounge with a welcome can of beer. It clambered up onto Stephen's lap and nuzzled into him, and he talked softly whilst stroking its head and ruffling its ears as they watched Newcastle beat Everton 4-0 in Round 6 of the FA Cup.

'I think you might bring us some good luck!' he said as Shearer scored the fourth in the 81st minute.

After rest and recuperation, Stephen put the pup in the bath and gave him the first decent wash he'd ever had, and what emerged was a less straggly and quite beautiful dog. Over the rest of the day the first tentative seeds of the incredible, ancient bond between man and canine, were sown. On Monday morning however, the man had to return to work whilst the canine stayed home alone.

Six

SHAK

Returning home on Monday evening after a long, busy day at work, catching up on things he'd postponed on Saturday whilst planning his Sunday trip to the shelter, Stephen found one of his tee-shirts not in the laundry basket where he'd tossed it, but lying in the hallway full of holes. The pup came charging through like an attack-dog, collided with Stephen's leg in its blind excitement, and jumped up and down in attempts to get as close to him as possible. Stephen took it out into the back lane as luckily it hadn't relieved itself in the house, but on the way back it paused to sniff at the corner of the sofa which it had ripped open earlier in the day. Stephen had a look, shrugged and thought, well at least the sofa's second hand and I'm sure I can stitch it up.

He fed the dog and it fell instantly asleep in his lap, apparently happy and content. It never attempted to chew anything for the rest of the evening, and Stephen concluded that the cause of it was his absence all day. Well he couldn't give up work, or take the dog with him, so would have to find some other solution to the problem. Next day he asked around the office for ideas, and repeatedly received a unanimous - 'Get rid of the bloody animal if it can't behave itself.'

But Stephen knew the dog could behave itself, at least when he was with it. That night when he got home, the pup had ripped the carpet at the bottom of the stairs, and the underlay, and Stephen collected rugs and vases from around the house to cover up the holes. He noted that almost all the damage was in the front hallway, which is where the pup always saw him last before disappearing.

Next night the pup had ripped out a few more pieces of carpet, dragged the rugs into a pile and chewed the edge of the stairs' newel post, but was excited when his new friend arrived home. At the weekend Stephen removed the hall carpet, replaced it with wooden floor tiles, and on Monday evening found them scattered through the house. He re-fitted the tiles and stuck them down with industrial-strength adhesive, and the pup chewed a lump out of the front door in apparent retaliation. Stephen had the door repaired and the pup gnawed a new chunk out of it.

It was beginning to look like a lost battle and Stephen

understood how easy it would be to take his colleagues' advice to get rid of the dog. He never even considered it though and as with every other problem in his life, was ever-more determined to solve it.

He was certain the animal's behaviour stemmed from being alone for long periods, and although growing quickly it was still very much a puppy - a baby which had suffered early separation from its mother, weeks alone as a stray on the streets, and then months of isolated incarceration in a metal cage - no wonder it was worried about being deserted by the person who'd finally rescued it from all that!

Stephen spoke to his mother about the difficulties he was encountering, and once she'd ascertained that the pup was staying whatever happened, made a suggestion:

'What about a dog-behaviour expert?'

'It's an idea but what's it gonna cost?'

'Look Stephen, you're my only son and if this is what you want, I'd like to help.'

'Yeah?'

'Yes, so I'll look into it and get things arranged, alright?'

'Okay, if you're sure.'

So a canine-behaviourist got involved, told them the dog was suffering from completely normal separation anxiety, which gave an official name to what Stephen already knew was happening. The guy made several suggestions, such as leaving a piece of Stephen's clothing with the dog when it was alone, which had a limited effect. Most suggestions didn't but one very positive factor did arise from Joan's involvement: her new husband, Keith, was working as a night-watchman and invited Stephen to drop the dog off each evening before he left for work. Patrolling through the night with Keith dramatically improved the pup's behaviour.

'He's full of energy, that's all,' said Keith. 'He's not a bad dog at all - just lonely and bored and missing his best friend, which is not surprising considering what the little fella's been through in his short life.'

The pup had turned the proverbial corner. Its behaviour continued to improve as confidence grew, and as it came to realise that Stephen would always come home, it stopped chewing and tearing stuff up and at last, Stephen was able to relax.

St Patrick's Day fell shortly after Stephen brought the pup home, which was now thriving on a special diet to make up ground after its poor start to life. They went out for a longer walk than usual, stopping at The Beacon pub near the West Monkseaton Metro station. They sat outside in the sunshine and as Stephen sipped a cold Guinness in honour of the Irish, the pup watched him keenly until it was offered a little taste. It loved the flavour and was soon draining more from its own half-pint glass.

'Well,' Stephen said. 'Now we're out drinking together on Paddy's day, suppose I'd better think of a proper name for you.'

Stephen acquired a taste for Guinness on trips to watch Glasgow Celtic play football. For many Tynesiders there's an affinity between Newcastle and Celtic supporters, and also Rangers depending which religious doctrine was preferred. Stephen wasn't particularly religious but appreciated the hardships the thousands of Irish immigrants who actually started many northern football clubs, had struggled to overcome after horrific famines and destitution drove them all over the world seeking better lives. He was first taken to a Celtic match by his father, and was immediately struck by the passion of Scottish supporters and the awesome atmosphere at Glasgow matches. Soon he was attending every home game at Celtic Park and eventually bought a season ticket. He loved the green-hooped strip and bought himself a shirt, but kept it in his bedroom most of the time, hanging on the wall next to the equally famous black and white stripes of 'The Magpies'.

Stephen loved good literature and read as much as he could. In a report on the Los Angeles riots after Rodney King's death at the hands of the police, he came across an American named Shakur which he was told meant: Thankful. He was thankful he'd been able to rescue his dog, thankful that the dog was now a major part of his life, and he knew the dog was thankful to him for giving it a future. The name seemed appropriate but Shakur didn't sound quite right for a German Shepherd. He wanted something unusual though so shortened it to Shak, and the little pup now had a name.

Stephen was still working until 8pm most nights to finance home-ownership, and Shak was a boisterous young dog not ideally suited to being locked in the house for 12 hours most days. One recommendation to stop any household damage re-occurring was to lock him in a crate.

'A crate?' he responded. 'You mean a cage? I brought him home to live with me and keep him out of cages.'

He refused to restrict Shak in such a way and as an alternative asked girlfriend Ronda to help out. She called around each lunchtime and took the dog out for a walk, which definitely helped relieve the stress of separation. This was ideal throughout the summer months but as September turned into October, and then November, Stephen noticed how cold the house was on returning home at night and in consequence, how cold Shak was. He tried adjusting the central-heating to kick in for a period each day, but the energy bills soared and the house was still cold by the time he got home. He was also cold after being in the house for 10 minutes, so to warm them both up he began taking Shak straight out for a long walk around the estate and up to the pond near the perimeter gate. Pretty soon they ventured further to trek across the fields every evening, and as the nights began to close in Stephen took his new, significantly discounted night-vision camera along. He filmed Shak hurtling through the woods and open countryside, and the dog looked forward immensely to these nightly romps. It also learned that it could always rely on Stephen to provide them and everything else it needed, and settled down completely to a wonderful new life.

With Shak becoming such a major part of his world and financial demands starting to ease, Stephen's previous focus on working to earn as much as possible to stay afloat, began to take a back seat. He was able to relax more and enjoy the good things around him, and spend more time with his beloved dog. He decided to leave Sony and its increasing demands, and took a similar job with a new company - Tomorrow's World, based just off the 1058 Coast Road. The move meant a quicker, simpler commute, a normal 5-day working week and although the basic wage wasn't quite as good, the resultant lifestyle was much better. He was far happier and so was Shak, and they now had full weekends to enjoy their adventures together.

Tomorrow's World at the time was a relatively small company, and Stephen had big experience in selling all kinds of cutting-edge technology. Because of his knowledge he was soon partnered with Sales Manager - David, and together they specialised in the ever shifting field of mobile-telephone innovation. The market for these products grew and grew as the phones themselves evolved to be smaller and smaller. With so many global companies involved though, competition was fierce, and a confusing cloud of differing contracts descended upon the masses of worldwide customers, eagerly awaiting each new trend and fashionable addition.

Stephen and David became more and more involved in putting together the myriad contract packages designed to hook every possible customer, and the owners of the company left them to it as they spent more time on foreign beaches, spending the resultant profits. Soon Stephen and David were virtually managing the whole company, and realising just how easy it all was to them.

The domestic technology market continued to grow, advertisements for able salespeople and managers abounded, and Stephen realised that he could probably progress further up the ranks if he switched companies.

'I think I might be ready to move on,' he told David one afternoon as they counted the month's profits.

'Oh yeah, where to?'

'I dunno, there're so many outfits looking for people...I thought I might apply for a manager's job somewhere.'

'Right, so you fancy managing a company do you?'

'Well I fancy the extra money and Friday afternoons off, even though I don't play golf!' Stephen laughed.

David smiled. 'It's not as easy as it looks y'know?'

'No, I know but I've picked up quite a lot working with you, David. Don't you think I could do it?'

David turned to look directly at his colleague. 'Yes, I do actually. In fact I'm pretty certain you could.'

Stephen smiled. 'Well, there you go then!'

'But I might have a better idea.'

'For me, or you?'

'For both of us.'

'How do you mean?'

'I mean I think we should both pack it in here - and start up on our own!'

'Like, start our own company?'

'Yes, what do you think?'

'I think it's an absolutely brilliant idea, let's do it!'

'Let's have a think about it and meet up at the weekend - see if we can come up with a business plan?'

The world immediately looked brighter to Stephen who'd often dreamed of owning his own company, and even the weather improved. On Saturday morning he was up early and took Shak for a long run on the beach north of Seaton Sluice. He parked behind the sand dunes just east of the A193, and wandered along the coast into Blyth. He hadn't been there for years and was surprised by the hustle & bustle of the old port which had suffered so much after political decimation of the UK fishing industry.

42

The Saturday market was heaving and the streets thronged with shoppers of all ages, and just a few metres from the centre of town were a series of large, free car parks.

'Shoppers' paradise,' he said to Shak, trotting along obediently on his lead. 'What a prime place to start up a new business.'

The dog looked up at him, anticipating an instruction, but was distracted as they passed an open butcher's shop door. He followed his nose and padded inside, head in the air, attracted by the smell of fresh meat.

'Can't see you ever becoming a vegetarian, Shak,' Stephen commented as his arm was jerked by the abrupt change in direction, causing the leash to slip from his hand.

He went into the shop to retrieve his dog, grabbed him by the collar and led him outside, where he regained his grip on the leash. As they set off again on their tour of

Blyth before heading back to the car, he noticed a sign standing out from the others in Bowes Street. It was on the front window of a vacant shop and declared in big, bold lettering: To Let, with a telephone number underneath and the estate agent's name. He restrained Shak with one hand, took his mobile out with the other, and tapped the number into its memory.

'Well done, Shak boy,' he said to the dog, walking off along Delaval Terrace with a smile on his face.

Seven

LIFE and DEATH

'**O**kay,' said David as they emerged from a long conversation with the estate agent. 'We can get the shop but how do we fund the business?'

'I got a possible idea about that as well,' Stephen answered.

'Go on then, let's hear it?'

'Well, I noticed this article in the paper about finance for new businesses.'

'Yeah but have you seen the interest rates on business loans these days?'

'It's a low-interest loan.'

'Low interest, is there such a thing?'

'Yeah, for young people under thirty who want to start their own business.'

'Really?'

'Yep, it's from the Prince's Trust and we might be able to get up to five grand!'

'Five thousand?'

'Uh-hum.'

'Well I suppose that'd get us started. How do we go about it?'

They put together a business plan, filled in all the forms and sent them off, and eventually received £5,000 into their new company account. It was an exciting time without many worries because although they'd given up their jobs, very little of their own money was used and they were confident of success.

They were allotted an official mentor but didn't really need him, and actually knew more about the details of their chosen market than he did. They had contacts with most mainstream suppliers, knew all the marketing angles and also kept some customers who preferred to do business with them, to continue their successful relationships. They recruited additional clients such as building and double-glazing companies, with supply-and-maintain contracts on multiple products.

Blyth turned out to be an excellent choice for their base and retail outlet, because in addition to the nearby parking facilities and large shopping areas, there were no other telephone shops in town at that time. Argos sold phones but with little backup, and the two young entrepreneurs avoided sale-only on a pay-as-you-go basis, in favour of customised contacts which retained the client base and maximised income.

They re-decorated and fitted out the shop themselves, named it 'Voicemail – Your Local Mobile Specialist' and even invested some of their own funds despite Stephen's father asking repeatedly, 'Are you sure about all this?'

But they never had any serious doubts and it was too late to retreat anyway. They hit the ground running in their matching suits, shirts and ties, and never looked back. They were fully committed to the new venture, liked being self-employed and were excited about their future prospects.

Shortly after Voicemail was up and running, Stephen met Elaine one night in Whitley Bay and they started going out regularly together. She got on well with Shak and just about everywhere they went - so did the dog. One weekend they went to see The Editors in concert at Glasgow, where Stephen booked a pet-friendly hotel and Shak had a great time meeting all the staff, sampling the food and travelling up and down in the lifts.

Stephen was making good money, owned the house at Hadrian Park and half a telephone business, and was relatively successful. Elaine had a flat in Bedlington but as their relationship deepened, she moved in with Stephen. Finding the one-bed house a little small for their needs, they bought a two-bed cottage back in Bedlington village, a few miles west of Blyth. They rented out the house and flat and the income paid the mortgages with a little left over.

After a couple of years together they tied the knot and got married, and daughter Neve was born shortly afterwards on 1st May 2006. They were both overjoyed and extremely proud to be parents, and felt sure that nothing could ever spoil their happiness as a family.

Shak seemed to understand how important baby Neve was, and sat for hours next to the cot as if guarding her. Stephen took him out for a walk as usual one morning and while trotting along normally, enjoying the fresh air and exercise, he suddenly came to an abrupt halt and collapsed. Stephen rushed him to Crofts Vets in Blyth and as the nurse led him through to the intake area, Shak stopped and looked back at his friend for a long moment. Stephen's heart lurched with love for his dog but although he didn't know it at the time – all was not well.

He was kept at Crofts for four days, during which time it was discovered that the poor animal was suffering from lymphoma. He was operated on as an emergency to remove the cancerous tumour from his lymph gland, and Stephen received the critical telephone call saying that the operation had been successful, and that Shak was recovering without any problems. He was relieved beyond words that his beloved, seven year-old companion had survived. Unfortunately, post-operation tests and screening revealed that the cancer had already spread, and Shak died peacefully on 19th June, the month after his daughter was born.

Stephen was distraught and probably suffering mild shock, and realised that there were some things in life, often very important things, that were well beyond his control. Despite the birth of Neve, whom he loved above everything, the loss of Shak hurt him so much that he vowed to avoid such pain ever again in the future, by never having another dog.

Eight

OSKAR

The wound to Stephen's heart over losing Shak healed slowly as the rest of his life went along productively and prosperously, and he spent much of his spare time coaching and managing a local football team. It occupied but failed to satisfy him, he eventually admitted to himself, and one day as he passed the Weston shelter, his new Toyota Supra inevitably turned into the entrance and parked outside. He got out and walked in slowly, holding back tears of sadness at memories of Shak. He looked around and was tempted to take home every dog there, and it was perhaps fortunate that there wasn't much passenger room in the Toyota.

He realised though, just how much being around the dogs relaxed him and allowed him to feel better about life, even though before entering he'd felt certain that he was as happy as he could be in the circumstances. So wasn't he really happy, and if not why not? He had a beautiful wife and daughter and together they owned three properties. He was joint owner of a thriving business, enjoyed a small fleet of cars for his personal use and was still involved with football, so what more could he possibly want?

He felt confused and decided that it must be because of where he was, and that he was missing Shak so much, and maybe he was now ready for another canine friend? He called Elaine and asked what she thought about his strange predicament.

'I need something but can't figure out what it is?'

'I've no idea what you're talking about, Stephen.'

'Well...'

'Can I hear dogs barking in the background?'

'Yes.'

'Where are you?'

'I'm at the shelter.'

'So you're adopting another dog?'

'That's what I mean - I'm not sure, what do you think?'

'I, I don't know - do whatever you think is best for you.'

'Okay, see you both later.'

He walked slowly around the shelter, looking in at each dog and noting that no German Shepherds were present. The place seemed to be full of Staffordshire Bull Terriers because of their popularity and consequent over-breeding. They were great dogs and proven to be excellent around the home and with young children, and wouldn't require quite as much exercise as some other breeds. He finished his tour and went into Reception, where a different girl from the one he'd dealt with

51

previously stood behind the counter in exactly the same position.

'Hello,' she said with a smile. 'Can I help you?'

'Yes, er I'm thinking about adopting another dog because mine died recently.'

'Oh, I'm sorry.'

'And er, I was also thinking about maybe becoming a volunteer…do you need any volunteers?'

'Oh er, I don't think we do at the moment but I can take your details?'

He left his contact numbers and went home but over the coming weeks, browsed online for other volunteering opportunities. One day he came across the Peoples Animal Rescue & Rehoming Team, PARRT, based in Queen Street, Amble, 20 miles up the east coast but with a network which spread via volunteers working from home, across Newcastle, Tyne & Wear and Northumberland. After a few formalities he was enlisted, reshuffled his priorities and wedged in an hour of two at the end of each day which after training, involved visiting the homes of prospective adopters to ensure their suitability.

'This will allow me to be around dogs and help them, without becoming attached and too emotionally involved,' he explained to Elaine in an effort to convince himself that he'd made a good decision.

The operation was well organised and run by dedicated, caring people and Stephen was pleased to be a small part of it all. He had very little contact with any dogs though, once he'd progressed to carrying out home visits on his own, and although he derived some satisfaction from that particular part in re-homing many animals, it soon wasn't enough for him. His tactics hadn't succeeded and in fact working on behalf of so many

52

homeless dogs day after day, actually increased his need to have one of his own.

By now he'd realised that it would have to be another German Shepherd as he'd fallen in love with the breed through Shak, and one weekend searched online for any that needed a permanent home. He found one with Deerlake Kennels at Langley Moor in County Durham, which also ran a rescue service. He drove down the A1 that afternoon to find a beautiful, black & tan bitch waiting there. She was in good shape and engaged well with him, but hadn't been socialised or even exposed to small children. The kennel staff said she could be a little nervy at times and he called Elaine. She was understandably worried about the close contact that it and any dog they adopted, would have with the new baby.

'I'll need a few days to think about it, and talk it over with the wife if that's alright?' he asked the man in charge.

'Yes that's fine, I understand - it's a big decision to make.'

'Well thanks for your time today.'

'No problem, don't mention it. I've got your details so if anything more suitable comes up, I'll give you first option.'

A few days later Stephen got a call from a number he didn't recognise.

'Hello?' he answered.

'Oh hello, my name's Helen and I run a German Shepherd rescue at Hamsterley Hall.'

'Oh right, over by Rowlands Gill.'

'Yes that's right, do you know the place?'

'I know the general area well enough.'

'Well I was speaking to Deerlake Kennels and they gave me your number.'

'Oh, I see.'

'Yes, so I thought I'd give you a call because we have a German Shepherd in, and I believe you might be looking for one, is that right?'

'Yes, that is right.'

'Well he's a three year-old male, if you're interested?'

'Three years old, you say?' Stephen asked, recalling how much fun he'd had with Shak as a puppy.

'Yes, three years old but with an extremely good temperament, and he's been around children all his life.'

'Really, so he's not a stray then?'

'No, unfortunately his owner has been diagnosed with multiple-sclerosis and is undergoing intensive treatment. He can't look after Oscar properly now and wants him to have a better life than he can provide.'

'That's such a shame for both of them.'

'Isn't it just.'

Stephen drove down to the roomy, 18th century Gothic country house next day to meet the dog. Within minutes he knew he wanted to take Oscar, and Helen arranged a staff visit to his home to make sure the domestic situation was suitable. No problems were identified at any point and the visit went well, and as the final hurdle he discussed the prospect in depth with Elaine, to make certain she was happy with his plans. She didn't object after he reassured her about Neve's safety, and two days later he returned to Hamsterley to collect the new family member.

'Oscar,' Stephen said to the dog as it sat on the lounge rug, looking keenly up at him. 'I like the name and it suits you, but I hope you won't mind if I alter the spelling slightly in honour of my old friend Shak?'

The dog wagged its tail and showed no objection.

'Thank you, Oskar.'

Hamsterley Hall.

Neve and Oskar

Nine

TRAPPED

At work things weren't going so well. Doing the same tasks day after day for 6 years had turned from exciting to boring, and then frustrating. The big retailers such as Orange and T-Mobile decided they weren't making enough profit, and upped the contract requirements from their subsidiaries. They also increased sales by media advertising and launching their own teams onto the high street, in direct competition with their independent agents such as Voicemail.

On more than one occasion whilst trying to solve customer problems, Stephen had to contact retailer network staff who then took over the situation by talking directly to the customers, switching them to new and totally different direct contracts and cutting Voicemail out of the whole procedure, whilst the customers sat in the Voicemail shop!

Previous Christmas periods had been taken up at Voicemail mainly by Argos customers, coming in with problems or for advice about presents they'd received, simply because it was possible to talk directly to an expert whereas it wasn't at the big retailer. Stephen and David always responded positively and politely, despite their time being used up for no payment by people who weren't even their customers!

So as Christmas approached again they decided not to open for the two weeks holiday period, and Stephen was more than happy to forget telephones for a short while. After the family festivities he found himself browsing the internet and always ended up looking at animal rescue sites. He still enjoyed helping to re-home dogs but wanted more direct involvement with them, as opposed to the people who adopted them. He studied pictures and facts online, noting information relating to as many breeds and types as he could, and slowly built his overall knowledge.

One afternoon he received a call from a friend asking, 'Hi Stephen, I believe you're running a dog rescue place now?'

'Ha ha, no I'm not running the place, I just help out a bit.'

'Yeah, that's what I meant, because one of my colleagues' sons was coming home from football training the other night, and came across a gang of kids stoning a little puppy.'

'Stoning it?' Stephen asked, horrified.

'Yes, they had it curled up on the grass and were pelting stones at the poor thing.'

'Jesus Christ, what happened to it?'

'The lad chased the kids and took the puppy home. It seems alright, Sheila says, but they're looking for someone who can find a new home for it.'

'Okay, give me the address.'

Stephen collected the bruised Lurcher, made sure it was healthy and asked around by phone and internet if anyone was interested. Four days later he found a suitable home for the ten week-old pup, and felt immense satisfaction. Word soon got around and he received more calls from people trying to re-home animals, and he learned how to expand the website he'd previously set up for his own enjoyment when Shak was alive. He posted pictures and details of homeless dogs and the whole thing snowballed in a very short time.

As the Christmas break came to an end, after spending most of each day with his family and Oskar, he was getting that dreaded back-to-school feeling about returning to work. He buried his head in general reading about canine activities, diets, traits and common mistakes people made in all areas, and looked forward far more to his unpaid time with PARRT. Elaine watched him and smiled and didn't ask too many questions, until her husband told her he was afraid of being caught in a trap.

'A trap?' she asked.

'Yes, trapped into having to work in a shop for the rest of my life, doing a job that I think I'm beginning to hate because it's all about greed and people having every little thing that they want while...while...'

'While some animals don't even get the basics?'

'Yes, exactly,' he replied, realising for certain that he was very unhappy with his life away from home.

'But that's the world we all live in, isn't it?'

'Yes but do we have to? I'm totally sick of having to listen to people complaining about things that are beyond

58

my control. There was a guy came in the other week, eyes bulging and screaming: "I've lost millions 'cos of you - you've cost me millions!"

I knew he was talking bollocks but stayed calm and said, I'm sorry sir but the whole network's down and we have no control over it.

"I don't give a shit," the guy shouted. "I bought the damn phone from you so it's your responsibility."

It wasn't of course because the contract was with the main network not Voicemail, but I knew I was wasting my time trying to explain so again forced myself to be polite to someone who didn't deserve it, and for whom I had no respect whatsoever.'

'Sometimes life's just like that.'

'My life at work's always like that.'

His wife looked at him for a long moment, before turning and walking away. He was completely sick of it all, he decided in an instant - sick of the whole thing and sick of wasting his time on it. What was once a joy was now a distasteful chore that he didn't wish to subject himself to any longer. He followed Elaine into the kitchen with Oskar at his side and said to her, 'I don't know quite how to say this, but I'm seriously thinking of packing it in.'

'I'd gathered you haven't been happy there for a while,' Elaine replied, feeding a treat to Oskar.

'Oh right, so what do you think?'

'I think you should do whatever makes you happy; you only live once, as they say.'

'Really? So you won't mind if I kick it into touch?'

'No, it's up to you, as long as you can still support your home and family?'

'Oh yeah, of course, you and Neve will always come first.'

Ten

VOCATION

O n Monday morning he rang David to let him know the decision he'd made, they agreed a settlement figure for Stephen's share of the business and he never went back. He spent the next week improving his new website and bought the domain name: shak.org.uk. Although he had Neve to look after every day, with Elaine working as a consultant's secretary at Wansbeck Hospital, he was soon feeling lost and aimless and began searching for paid positions at dog sanctuaries.

He checked the shelters he knew plus rescue operations, vets and anywhere else he could think of, but after a week was becoming concerned as he realised that finding employment in his chosen field let alone obtaining it, was extremely difficult. He persevered though as always, refused to panic and eventually received a reply from the Weston Vale Animal Shelter on the western edge of Newcastle, where he'd found Shak. The letter asked him to attend for a half-day, unpaid suitability trial.

He attended the following Wednesday; it lasted just under three hours and he was surprised at the general fluidity of the internal operation. He also liked the environment and busy atmosphere as he filled in the required Health & Safety forms, before being allowed to get involved physically. He then had an interview with the Animal Welfare Manager - Lynda, who was pleasantly business-like, and then got kitted out with wellington-boots and overalls.

His first job was to carry stacks of donated, used newspapers from the storage area to the kennels, and spread them on the floors to absorb moisture. The floors had already been cleaned and he'd progress to that duty in good time if deemed worthy. He again felt immediate satisfaction from helping animals, and also the under-funded and under-staffed shelter. He felt great relief from being trussed up in a suit and tie all day - compared to the comfort and freedom of manual working gear.

After a couple of hours joyful drudgery a member of staff - Martin, appeared and pointed to a huge, black & tan Rottweiler standing in a cage looking at them. 'Can you take that one for a walk outside,' he said as an instruction.

'Okay,' Stephen replied with a smile. 'What's his name?'

'Er, Bruno I think. There's a leash hanging in the corridor.'

Stephen got the leash, clicked it onto the dog's collar and set off. As he reached the exit Martin shouted, 'Be careful, he doesn't like other dogs.'

He's going to take some holding if he decides to go for one, Stephen thought, feeling the massive power of the animal through the leash as he led it out into the central enclosure. There were several other dogs being exercised in the area by volunteers, and Stephen didn't want to mess up and fail the trial as he noticed Martin watching from the doorway.

He took firm hold of the leash which he kept short, and Bruno trotted along happily at his side. The dog was distracted by others around it but Stephen tweaked the lead to keep his attention, and the 20-minute session went well. Martin was nodding as he waved him back in and said, 'Lock him up again then report back to Lynda's office.'

He spent another 10 minutes stroking and talking to Bruno as a reward for his good behaviour, before going to see the manager.

'So how do you like it here?' she asked.

'I like it just fine,' he answered and they had a brief discussion about all the duties he'd be required to carry out - none of which sounded too difficult until right at the end:

'And what about euthanasia,' Lynda asked, looking up from her notes. 'How would you deal with that?'

'Erm, I realise I'd have to in extreme circumstances, but would hope I could find a suitable alternative for the dog so it didn't become necessary.'

She nodded and pursed her lips, and looked deep into the eyes of the applicant sitting in front of her.

'Alright,' she said. 'Let me have a think about things and we'll get back to you.'

He left feeling reasonably good about the day, and also about the hard, manual and unpaid work he'd done. Physical endeavour produces its own, unique rewards lost to so many over the centuries, and he was still buzzing when he arrived home to walk Oskar and Poppy - a Collie cross which had been with various members of Stephen's family before recently settling down with him.

A few days later he received a call from Lynda saying his trial had gone well, and she would contact him when the next vacancy came up.

'Oh, so there isn't a vacancy now?'

'No, not right now but we like to plan ahead.'

He put the phone down and flopped into an armchair, and felt like he'd been sitting there doing absolutely nothing when it rang again, two weeks later.

'Hello Stephen, can you start work on Monday at nine o'clock?'

'Yes, no problem.'

'Alright, we'll see you then.'

'Thank you Bruno,' he said out loud to himself. 'For getting me through the trial.'

He arrived early to start his new, minimum-wage job but had to wait half an hour as the previous holder of the post - was in the office being sacked! This might be more of a cut-throat place to work than I imagined, Stephen thought, but pushed it from his mind as he wriggled into wellies and waterproofs to shadow a series of fellow-workers. He was soon finding his feet and getting into the swing of things, and enjoying every minute.

Tuesdays were vet-visit days every week to check for kennel-cough, small wounds, infections and any other ailments, and Stephen was given the task of administering medication by mouth, but there was other veterinary work that required his presence, and he was summoned to help with three terminations.

'How do you feel about this?' Lynda asked as they sat outside the room where it would happen, and the vet tinkered with his lethal equipment inside.

'Not the best I've ever felt Lynda, but if it's got to be done I'll be glad when it's all over.'

'It doesn't take long at all,' she said, as if describing some mundane office procedure.

65

Eleven

THE KILL ROOM

All too soon it was time to enter the small room which was stark, cold, lit by a glaring overhead strip-light, and resembled a public toilet more than a place for surgical procedure. Martin followed with another member of staff, dragging a dog between them. It was a big, powerful specimen but couldn't stand on its own without assistance. It kept stumbling or falling to one side or the other, which annoyed Martin who used his knee to bring it alongside the metal table. As it turned they gripped each end of its body, and Stephen gasped in horror when he realised it was a Rottweiler.

'What's the matter with it?' he asked Lynda in alarm.

'It's been given a dose of ACP to sedate it.'

'ACP?'

'Yes, acetylpromazine.'

'But that's known to increase anxiety isn't it?'

'It doesn't matter Stephen, now pay attention to the procedure.'

The two men hoisted the drugged animal onto the table and forcibly held it down as the vet moved in with his killing equipment. Stephen's legs suddenly lost their strength and he slid down the wall until his knees hit the floor and there, with his eyeline on the same level as the dog, he recognised it. It was Bruno and its glazed stare focused on Stephen, looking at him as hope slithered away and the shelter workers tightened their grip. Martin held Bruno's arm tightly in a well-practised manner that pressurized the veins, causing them to protrude, and the vet injected two prepared needles, one straight after the other. Stephen gasped.

'It's a big dog,' explained Lynda. 'The injection is based on the weight of each animal and the vet can't always get enough in one needle.'

It was a horror film unfolding and Stephen was about to cry out in protest, when again he saw Bruno watching him, through eyes which slowly dimmed from the life of a proud young animal - to its needless death. Tears streamed down his face and he hung his head in shame at even being there - being present and not preventing the unwarranted murder of such a magnificent, noble animal that was bred to serve the needs and whims of man.

'How can you possibly justify that?' he gasped at Lynda.

'It couldn't be re-homed because it was dog-aggressive and a Rottweiler,' she replied with a puzzled frown.

'He wasn't, he wasn't aggressive, he was just nervous around other dogs and who knows for what reason. I could easily have sorted that out.'

Martin's assistant held a black plastic bin-liner open at the side of the table, and he pushed the dog inside, letting it fall to the floor with a lifeless thud. They then tied the bag and dragged Bruno out of the room, to stack him against the wall like general rubbish.

Stephen was unable to move or speak, and watched in continuing horror as a beautiful Collie was brought in to be dispatched and discarded as garbage, and then a young Staffie which still had the strength to resist, its paws scraping across the hard-tiled floor. It was just back from a failed re-homing so he'd had his chance, said Martin as he stacked the little, still-warm body on top of the previous two victims of the day's cull. Later that afternoon a van rolled up and the dead animals were thrown inside, and taken to a pet crematorium where they were stored until enough bodies accumulated to warrant a joint cremation.

Stephen was sickened and deeply resentful that he'd been made part of it all, but it didn't weaken his resolve. He never thought for one moment that he'd made a wrong choice, and instead was even more determined to change the system. In the meantime he'd make sure that no dogs under his control ever met the same ghastly, un-deserved end to life. To do so he'd have to make sure they were all re-homed before the deadly system scooped them up and consigned them to bin-liners.

Those thoughts and plans restored the drive that had died on the vine of the mobile-phone industry, and he immediately put it to good use. He returned to work the following day with renewed enthusiasm, which he knew surprised some of his colleagues who had witnessed his emotional breakdown the day before. He threw himself into every task and never took breaks, preferring to eat on the hoof than miss any opportunity to save a life. He used his salesmanship pro-actively by actually approaching visitors to the kennels and asking if he could help. None of the other staff did so and prospective adopters often commented that they would probably have left empty-handed if he hadn't offered his expert advice. Many were unsure which if any breed might suit their lifestyle, and were afraid of making a mistake. With Stephen's wealth of new-found knowledge and need to get all adoptions right first time, so that none were returned and became less adoptable as they grew older, no mistakes were made and very few visitors left without making applications.

'We've never re-homed so many in the same period before,' Lynda informed him with a smile after his first three months' service.

'Let's hope none of them come back,' he answered.

'None have so far so things are looking good, and we haven't had to put any down either to make room.'

'I know, and I'm definitely glad about that.'

'So you got over your initial shock then?'

'I got over the shock but I'll never get over the horror and sadness of it.'

'It takes time - you'll get used to it.'

'I don't want to get used to it Lynda, I want to change it.'

'Well you're on the right track, so keep up the good work.'

He did, and kept a record of his successes by photographing each dog and posting pictures on his website, with advice on how to handle possible problems with different breeds and types. Tips on exercise, food and diet, socialisation with people, children and other canines proved very popular and he became even more well known in the animal rescue world. People approached him directly for advice on adopting, and he took the time to give it gladly and in detail, in a further effort to reduce the number of unwanted animals.

He drew up a thick catalogue of abandoned Greyhounds, discarded in their hundreds after often successful racing careers, simply because they're not regarded as pets or even animals - but disposable financial commodities.

The birth date and lineage of every dog is recorded and listed by the Greyhound Board of Great Britain (GBGB), and marked by a tattoo on the inside ear of each animal. This information can be used to trace the history of often bedraggled strays back six or seven generations. The racing history of a dog often has a spellbinding effect on prospective adopters, who usually can't believe that even very successful racers are simply thrown out as rubbish once their competitive days are over. Stephen cashed in on this to re-home dozens of Greyhounds. He carried a file with him at all times so that he wasn't caught out at any point, knowing that even the slightest delay can scupper an adoption and ultimately - lead to euthanasia.

Discarded Greyhounds

Vet visit day at a 'shelter'

Unloved, unwanted and terrified

Twelve

THE KILL LIST

Stephen was struck by how just one incident report in the news could result in a flood of abandoned dogs, and he noticed it mostly in relation to Rottweilers. They are big, powerful dogs and it's easy to imagine them as dangerous animals, but the facts are that they're a very stable, hardworking breed originally used in the German town of Rottweil, as herders and to pull merchants' carts, being much cheaper to buy and keep than horses, ponies or donkeys. Inaccurate news reports and incapable owners quickly endowed them with an undeserved reputation, which made the breed almost impossible to re-home at various times, and Stephen dedicated much of his time to discovering the true nature of Rottweilers to pass on the information. Other rescue staff both from his own shelter and others up and down the country began contacting him for advice. Many couldn't understand why Rottweilers were taken into shelters in the first place, with most establishments adhering to the policy that they were too dangerous to be re-homed.

'We take them in and put them to sleep a week later,' said Jenny in exasperation from a shelter in Yorkshire. 'What's the point?'

'The week is the point,' replied Stephen.

'How come?'

'The shelters get paid by the local authority to take them in off the street, but they only have to keep them for seven days in case an owner shows up.'

'So it's just about the money and we have no intention of re-homing them?'

'I'm afraid so, in fact most shelters at the moment have active policies not to re-home, but of course the alternative is to leave them out on the streets.'

'It's still disgusting.'

Rottweilers became a special case for Stephen, initially ignited by what happened to innocent Bruno, and he became an ardent advocate for them. Soon he was receiving requests for advice from rescuers all over the country. One Monday morning he arrived at work to find an underweight female Rotty in one of his allotted kennels.

'Have we got any of her history?' he asked Martin.

'No, she was left tied to a lamp-post a week ago but it doesn't matter - she's on the kill-list for tomorrow. I only put her in your kennel because it's empty at the moment.'

Stephen stormed off to Lynda's office and shouted, 'There's a female Rotty in one of my pens but Martin says she's on the kill-list!'

'Yes, we've had her seven days Stephen, and you know it's our official policy not to re-home Rottweilers.'

'I'm re-homing them.'

'Unofficially.'

'So give me a chance with her Lynda, I know I can help her.'

'There's nothing I can do now…'

'I can get her to a no-kill shelter - you've had your seven-day payment for her so let me at least try?'

Lynda was stung by the payment remark and avoided further eye contact. 'I've nothing more to say on the matter. You can bring it up at today's staff meeting if you like, but that's all you can do.'

He attended the meeting, put forward his case but was fobbed off with rules, policies, lack of space and dangers to the public.

'Look,' he pleaded. 'I understand that you have limited funds and are always short of kennel-space, and if an animal is truly dangerous you have little choice, but this bitch hasn't even been fully assessed yet.'

'She's been through the system,' intervened Martin. 'So there's no other option.'

'Let me at least try?'

'No,' Martin shouted. 'She's on the list for tomorrow and that's that.'

Stephen's anger and frustration rose like an erupting volcano as he stood and hissed, 'I am not listening to this bullshit any longer - there is no excuse for what you're doing and I will not stand by and watch it happen.'

'What exactly do you mean by that, Stephen?' asked Lynda.

'I'm going to the newspapers,' he said calmly, walking out and slamming the door behind him.

As he got into the car his mobile buzzed. It was Lynda.

'Alright Stephen, you've made your point. We can give you another week with her but that is definitely all, and if nothing changes within that week - it's over, okay?'

He telephoned a kennel he'd spoken to a few times before based at Embleton, just off the B1339 and a few miles south of Bamburgh Castle, with the Farne Islands offshore to the east.

'Any chance you could hold a Rottweiler bitch for me until I get her re-homed? She's on death-row at the moment.'

'We can probably find space, and might even be able to get a home for her depending on how she presents, but you'd have to bring her to us - we can't collect from another shelter especially if they've already claimed the seven-day payment.'

'Oh, right, er...okay.'

Thirteen

ROWENA

On Friday morning Stephen walked into Lynda's office and handed her two A4 sheets of paper.

'What's this?' she asked.

'I've carried out a full assessment of Rowena and that's my report with final recommendation.'

'Ro…Rowena, which one's that?'

'The Rotty bitch.'

'The…oh, I see,' she said with resignation, scanning the two pages of neat typing. 'So what's the result?'

'She's fine, no serious problems that affect her behaviour, and I've recommended her for re-homing to an experienced adopter.'

'Our policy is not to re-home to members of the public Stephen and anyway - you've only got two days left before the deadline.'

'I've read the policy thoroughly Lynda, and if a request is made by an experienced handler who guarantees that the dog will never be placed in a position where it can cause harm - you should let it go.'

She studied him for a second or two. 'You're taking this one very seriously,' she said, laying his report on her desk.

'I take them all seriously, and this one's a matter of life or death.'

She paused again. 'Alright, fine, have it your way but as I said, the deadline runs out on Monday - one day before the vet's next visit.'

'Well at least she's got a chance.'

'A very slim one.'

'Are you er...are you working this weekend, Lynda?'

'Just Saturday morning why, aren't you?'

'Of course - as you say, I've only got two days.'

She shook her head. 'You're wasting your time, Stephen.'

'Maybe but just in case, can you be sure to put a note in the diary that Rowena's been passed for re-homing?'

She looked at him directly for a few seconds. 'Okay, alright I'll note it in the diary but I warn you now - there can be no further extension to the deadline and as of Monday - she's back on the list.'

'Thank you for that at least, Lynda.'

On Sunday morning staff were thin on the ground and at break time, a well-dressed man walked into the pens area, spoke briefly to Stephen and followed his directions back to Reception. Stephen followed him and said to the receptionist, 'Hi Paula, this gentleman wants to adopt Rowena - the Rottweiler in Pen 7. I've checked everything out; he's very experienced with the breed and has already paid the fee.'

He placed five £20 notes on the counter along with a sheet signed off by himself and the applicant, as Paula replied, 'Oh, I didn't think Rotties were available for re-homing.'

'Yeah, she was made available on Friday after re-assessment, and Lynda's recorded it in the main diary if you want to check?'

'Er, no, no if you say it's okay that's good enough for me, Stephen,' Paula answered, picking up the money and sliding the form to one side.

Stephen led Rowena out to the man's expensive car, parked right out front, and Paula stood in the doorway watching them.

'Well thanks for all your help,' the adopter said, flicking a dog hair from his pristine, pin-striped suit. 'Give me a call anytime you want to check how she's doing,' he added, smiling back at Paula.

'I'll do that,' Stephen confirmed. 'In fact I could call around tomorrow afternoon to er, make sure she's settled in alright?'

'Tomorrow afternoon?'

'Yeah, about half four?'

'Yes that'll be alright, I'll see you then.'

At 17.30 the following day Stephen delivered a female Rottweiler to the Embleton sanctuary, where she stayed for seventeen days before being re-homed with a family in Glasgow. Stephen drove her there himself, met the adopters and made sure she and all concerned were happy.

Two weeks later he got a call from a shelter in Oxford. 'Hi,' the caller said. 'I believe you rescue condemned Rottweilers?'

'I rescue all condemned dogs if I can but yes, Rottweilers are having a particularly rough time at the moment.'

'Aren't they just. Well look, we've had a call from a resident in Darlington which is a lot closer to you than us, about a Rottweiler that's been used as a guard-dog and left chained up in a yard, apparently abandoned.'

'Okay, give me the address and I'll check it out.'

Stephen rescued the half-starved dog from being tethered in a pen which was open to all weather conditions, and took it to Embleton from where after assessment, it also was re-homed.

'Well thanks to Embleton that's two dogs that would be dead by now if we hadn't intervened,' Stephen said to Elaine over a Saturday night curry.

'That's great,' she replied with a smile, tearing off a piece of naan bread. 'It's obviously making you happy and given you back your zest for life.'

Fourteen

CHARITY

SHAK

Safe Homes And Kindness

Every dog that Stephen rescued to Embleton cost him £5 per day from his own pocket, and money soon became a major problem. Local people knew by now what he was trying to do though, and began supporting him by donating small amounts directly by hand each week, in social settings and particularly at football venues. He was still operating as a player/manager and news of his ventures spread from team to team across the region. At a post-match evening it came to light that one of the players' mothers was ill with breast-cancer, and it was decided to stage a series of events in support of research. Knowing that many research organisations fund horrific and unnecessary experiments on animals, Stephen selected *Breast Cancer UK* which he knew did not.

Whilst brain-storming with Elaine for additional fund-raising ideas she reminded him that she was partway through a beauty treatment course, and volunteered to carry out a sponsored chest-wax at a suitable venue. Stephen put the word out and centre-forward Tony asked, 'So what you having waxed then, Stephen? You're the manager so you gotta do something special.'

'Nah, I'm not into that. Don't mind organising it but I got sensitive skin.'

'Don't be soft, get out there and get waxed.'

'You can go wax my arse.'

'Brilliant idea!'

And that's what happened, in public under spotlights at the Bedlington Terrier public house, and donations flooded in amongst the laughter and applause. All takings were passed on to the charity and shortly afterwards, Stephen was approached by a woman called Margaret, holding a folded envelope.

'What's this?' he asked.

'It's a hundred pounds,' she answered, holding it out to him.

'What's it for?'

'It's for charity.'

'Oh right, for breast-cancer?'

'No, for your charity.'

'Really?'

'Yes, I know you raise money for charity because I've seen you doing it - quite a lot of you in fact!' she replied with a broad smile.

'Oh dear,' he said, feeling his face burn.

'And I know you've been spending your own money saving condemned dogs.'

'How did you know about that?'

'Two of the volunteers from Weston Vale did some work on my fences at home, so I could adopt my little Gracie. I offered them a hundred pounds but they refused and told me about you instead, so here I am!'

'Well that's very nice of you, thank you very much.'

'I'm telling as many people as possible about you as well.'

'Really?'

'Yes, so hopefully you'll be getting more donations soon.'

'Wow, I better get something official set up so people know exactly where their donations are going.'

Stephen realised he needed a more formal approach to funding if he was really going to start a new venture, so took Maggie's £100 to the TSB where he kept funds related to the football team. He told a young lady with a faded name-badge that he wished to open a separate charity account, and after a short wait was shown into a small side-office.

'It must all be very exciting,' said a slightly older lady when he explained his plans.

Stephen smiled and nodded as she spread a range of forms on the desk between them.

'So to start with,' she continued, clicking her ballpoint into action. 'What's the name of the charity?'

'It's er, it's…Shak.'

'S, h…'

'S, h, a, k.'

'Right, what does that stand for?'

'Oh er, it stands for ... Safe ... Safe Homes and ... Kindness. Safe Homes And Kindness, does that sound alright?'

'It sounds fine, Mr Wylie,' she replied with a smile, jotting the name down at the top of the first form.

He answered a range of further questions, signed his name half a dozen times and laid the ballpoint down in perfect alignment with the edge of the last form. 'Is that it?' he asked hopefully.

'Yes, all done and dusted and Shak is now an official charity once you register it with the Commission.'

'Right, well thank you very much,' Stephen said, standing and holding out his hand.

'No problem at all and thank you for using our services again. Hope all goes well with your new venture and we'll send you monthly statements for tax purposes, and so you can demonstrate that donations are kept separate from your personal or any other funds.'

That was one of the main reasons for opening the account but in fact, Stephen had often daydreamed about setting up his own shelter. So now he thought about that prospect again, more seriously this time, and decided that following his recent painful experiences at Weston Vale he didn't want a place like that. No, he had a different, quite radical idea which matched his personality perfectly. He wanted to give permanent sanctuary not temporary shelter - to dogs condemned to death for no good reason and guarantee their moral right to a good life.

He hadn't yet thought through what he would actually do with the animals once rescued, particularly as many would bring quite serious behavioural problems with them, but was determined and confident that he could at least keep the innocent, maltreated animals alive and free from suffering - if he had somewhere to do it.

A badly reported incident involving a Rottweiler in late 2006, led to a flurry of sensationalised news reports, all accompanied by photographs of completely different dogs, snarling, teeth-bared on the front pages, which in turn led to a spate of abandoned Rottweilers and one soon landed up at Weston Vale.

A young bitch officially described as dog-aggressive with a volatile fear of strangers, was immediately listed for imposed death but Stephen begged for one week to prove otherwise. Based on his previous success he was granted the week and at the end of it, Welfare Manager, Lynda left on a 3-month secondment elsewhere in the country. Her duties were assumed by General Manager, Charles who noticed Stephen coming into Reception that afternoon.

'Stephen,' he shouted.

Stephen stopped and the two dogs he'd been walking together sat obediently side by side.

'Times up on the aggressive Rottweiler bitch.'

'I know.'

'Right, so where is she?'

'She's right here,' Stephen answered, nodding at the dogs.

Charles was astonished at the change in the Rottweiler, realised at last that Stephen was competent and could fulfil his promises, and immediately took him far more seriously than biased reports on his past actions had previously allowed. Stephen successfully re-homed the dog and shortly afterwards was called into the office by Charles, who asked if he was prepared to take over Lynda's duties for the remainder of her secondment.

Stephen knew the appointment was temporary but that it would equip him for more senior roles in the future, so agreed.

'As long as I have the power to make and act on decisions I believe to be correct, as Lynda would?'

'That's an essential part of the job but of course it'll all be very much on a trial basis to start with.'

Fifteen

GUILT

Stephen got straight to work, employing his new authority to good effect by establishing possible escape routes for condemned dogs, and planning ahead so the euthanasia option arose less often. He looked for opportunities to bring in extra funding by utilising links with the news media.

On one occasion a frightened, nervous and defensively aggressive Jack Russell was brought in after being found lying next to its dead owner for three days. Stephen immediately saw a news opportunity and as the dog was now in danger because of its behaviour, he felt justified in using the tragic circumstances of its owner's death for such a purpose. After a few days care and attention the Jack Russell calmed down, became easy to handle and appeared on local television with two girls from the shelter making a fuss of him.

One of Stephen's new responsibilities would be supervising the weekly vet's visit, including listed terminations. He was very nervous and reluctant to even be in the same room after his traumatic experience with Bruno, but things got even worse when Charles suggested he should take Martin's place in holding a dog for lethal injection, to demonstrate the procedure as part of staff training. He was fully prepared to flatly refuse but reasoned with himself that it would happen anyway; that if he refused he'd almost certainly lose his new powers, and also the opportunity to actually change the approach of shelter staff and save more lives in the long run.

A Staffordshire Bull Terrier had been listed because she'd contracted kennel-cough which wasn't clearing up. Stephen told himself again that if he assisted in the sacrifice of this one dog - it would allow him to carry on saving many others, so knowing that he was still very much on trial in his new position he agreed to do it. Forcing himself to hold the struggling dog on the killing table, he twisted her trembling flesh so that the veins protruded, watched her die with tears in his eyes, but at least carried her out of that horror-room with some dignity afterwards. The experience crushed and disgusted him and he vowed to never again take part under any circumstances, but would carry the guilt with him forever.

He bitterly regretted allowing himself to be cajoled into the execution of an innocent animal which had previously learned to love and trust people, and immediately lodged a formal complaint about the killing process and the effects on staff forced to be involved in it. He questioned its morality, legality and whether the shelter was responsible for mentally injurious actions towards its employees and volunteers. He was summoned to Charles' office the very same day.

'I'm afraid things aren't working out as well as we'd hoped,' the General Manager announced, keeping his eyes on the desk in front of him.

'Oh?'

'No, some of the staff seem unclear about certain aspects of their duties, which has led to a need for extra hands on deck, more in line with how things were before…'

'Before you asked me to take over as Animal Welfare Manager?'

'On a temporary trial basis, I must remind you but yes, that's about the size of it.'

'So where does that leave us?'

'It leaves us with a problem to which the only immediate remedy is for you to return to your previous duties, I'm afraid.'

'And what about the AWM duties?'

'Well, you could carry on in both positions if you wish to help us out on a voluntary basis?'

'Both positions?'

'Yes.'

'On a voluntary basis?'

'Uh-hum, that would work best for the shelter.'

'Are you joking, Charles?'

'No Stephen, I'm afraid I'm not joking.'

'There's no way one person can do both jobs.'

'Perhaps if you contained yourself to your stipulated duties and not to placing the whole organisation in jeopardy?'

'Jeopardy?'

'That's the effect your persistent quest for changes is having.'

'That's because change is very necessary and long overdue, and not being addressed.'

'We seemed to be jogging along quite nicely before you er…before your involvement.'

'Jogging along - slaughtering innocent animals every week?'

'That's incorrect and uncalled for Stephen; you know as well as I do that it's sometimes necessary to…'

'I know nothing of the sort, unless you class clearing kennel space as fast as possible to increase income a necessity?'

Charles remained silent, fingers twitching and eyes blinking rapidly.

'And you want me to shut up about that and do what I'm told, is that it?' Stephen continued.

Charles slapped a palm to his desk in anger. 'I want you to assist in the running of the centre along established lines without creating additional, unnecessary problems for us.'

'Right, well in my opinion the changes I'm pushing for are extremely necessary and there is no way I can do two jobs at once.'

'In that case, you leave me no option but to withdraw the AWM offer and ask you to return to your previous duties.'

That conversation signalled the beginning of the end of Stephen's career at Weston Vale. He felt used and abused and guilty about his complicity in the Staffie's execution. He was also angry and disillusioned with the whole animal rescue system, which disallowed knowledgeable, frontline staff to have any effect on it despite their good intentions. It's possible therefore, that he wasn't in the most positive mood or mindset when he clashed with a long-standing staff member:

Susan had worked at the shelter for years and knew the system inside out, and used that accrued knowledge to her exclusive benefit on occasion. Such opportunities arose most weekends and especially bank holidays, after members of the public left donations of food and other items at the entrance when the shelter was closed. There was no procedure for sharing these gifts amongst all the animals equally, and Susan took full advantage in claiming them all for her charges by arriving at work very early. Stephen objected reasonably politely one day, but Susan was confident because she was constantly praised by management for her quiet, non-disruptive and non-questioning efficiency, and shouted him down. A heated argument ensued and when Charles later intervened on her behalf, Stephen suddenly realised that it was over - he'd had enough of Weston Vale and announced that he was leaving. Despite his previous conversation with Charles, Stephen had continued to carry out some of the AWM duties in addition to his own to keep things going but now, a replacement Welfare Manager, Sheila, was shipped in.

'So what will you do now?' she asked Stephen after a few days when they were getting on with each other surprisingly well.

'I'm not sure, Sheila. I hadn't planned to leave so soon but I just can't stay here any longer.'

'Are you changing direction altogether?'

'Oh no, I still want to help animals, just not the way it's done here.'

'Well it's obvious you're good at what you do from what I can see, and your heart's definitely in the right place.'

'Fat lot of good it's done me.'

'Well I know Lucy, the owner of East Meadow rescue is looking for experienced staff.'

'Oh yeah, who're they?'

'It's a private kennel but they rent out space to the RSPCA for their rescues as well.'

'Right, that might be interesting,' Stephen responded but without much enthusiasm.

'Well I'll leave her number on my desk just in case you want to give her a call.'

When he got home that night he took Oskar out for a long, two-hour walk along Shak's old favourite route, and thought long and hard about his future. He had to admit he was interested in the RSPCA - it was by far the biggest rescue organisation in the country so maybe he could learn something? Next morning he got to work early, picked up the East Meadow number from Sheila's desk, and put it in his pocket.

Sixteen

SASHA

Stephen got home, took Oskar for his usual walk and then made the call to East Meadow. He was invited for interview and immediately noted the different atmosphere. It was less noisy and manic and not really like a shelter, and had varied animal species. The interview was very informal, carried out in the kitchen.

'So why did you leave your last position?' asked Lucy after ten minutes of general questions.

'There er, there were policies in operation that I just couldn't agree with.'

'Did they involve the euthanasia process?'

'Yes, they did, I went there to help animals not kill them for no reason.'

Lucy nodded. 'Don't worry, I understand, it can be quite horrific can't it.'

He nodded in agreement. 'So I was very pleased when Sheila told me about you.'

Lucy smiled and nodded again. 'Alright,' she said, folding her notebook. 'We'll let you know as soon as we can, and thank you for coming along today.'

Stephen left with mixed feelings about his prospects but two hours later Lucy called him. 'Can you start work for us tomorrow, Stephen?'

'Yes, yes I can and thank you for the opportunity.'

He was happy to leave the sour situation at Weston Vale and telephoned Sheila to thank her, as Lucy had obviously asked for a reference. She was pleased but sad to see him go, knowing he'd rebelled against Weston's systems for the best reasons.

His first day at East Meadow went well and he met all the other staff, which comprised four young females. He was given basic duties cleaning kennels and walking dogs in the private section by Kennel Manager, Tracy, but was not allowed into the RSPCA pens. This area housed animals rescued from inadequate or abusive situations, all pending court cases, and though Stephen showed immediate interest and had expressed curiosity at the interview, Tracy was overly protective of the whole operation and kept him out. She made it very clear that she did not appreciate his interest, which meant he had to be careful not to invoke her wrath - always simmering just below the surface of her complicated personality.

After just a few days she began to display actual animosity towards Stephen on occasion, and her attitude soon spread to the other staff who began whispering to each other when he was around. He was aware that he might seem a bit odd to the young women, all in their twenties while he was a thirty-something male who came to work in one of three expensive cars left over from his career with Voicemail, but he discovered that there was another dimension to their apparent prejudice.

'Oh no, not already,' said Sheila with a sigh during a catch-up telephone call over the weekend.

'How do you mean?' he asked. 'Not already what?'

'Well Stephen, let's just say that Tracy and her girls have...how should I put it...a very close relationship?'

'You mean because they've been working together for a long time?'

'Closer than that.'

'Closer than...do you mean...?'

'Uh-hum.'

'Right, well that's okay, I don't have a problem with that.'

'No but they might have a problem with you, right?'

'Well yeah, they certainly seem to.'

'You're obviously not being subservient enough for them, and neither should you have to be.'

'So, are they all in this...relationship?'

'Well three of them certainly are. I'm not sure about the fourth. I was hoping Lucy had sorted out the problems that have arisen in the past by now, but apparently not.'

'I'm never going to be allowed to fit in there am I?'

'Not unless you behave exactly as they want you to.'

'Which is?'

'Do what they tell you and keep quiet.'

'So I just bag the crap, walk the dogs and keep my stupid mouth shut?'

'That's about the size of it, I'm afraid.'

He tried again to fit in with the unofficial hierarchy but couldn't because he wasn't allowed to. As an alternative he kept his head down, mouth closed and made sure his work was always beyond reproach, but the girls obviously saw that as weakness and steadily piled on the pressure to oust him from his job. They effectively began to hound him out in a reverse witch-hunt, but Stephen refused to give in - he was working in a sector where he really wanted to be, had made significant sacrifices to be there and had nowhere else to go, so carried on as best he could under very unfavourable circumstances. Perhaps he had to battle through these tests and trials to reach his goals, he wondered? Maybe he had to prove himself worthy and qualify before he could make a real difference to the lives of suffering animals? Well, he would not be found wanting in the perseverance department, he decided.

He threw himself into his work, caring as much as possible for the animals he was allowed access to, including cats, dogs, rabbits, ferrets, goats and pigs. He was routinely given the tasks of cleaning out the pigsty and washing the goats' hooves before clipping, during which he was always instructed to hold their hind legs. The goats were nervy during clipping and almost always relieved themselves during it.

'Well, it's easier for you to clean it off,' explained Tracy with affected seriousness, shaking her shoulder-length hair.

By now Stephen was certain that his time at East Meadow wouldn't be of long duration, so was determined to learn as much as possible, particularly about their re-homing process which was more gradual and thorough than at Weston Vale, but included checking prospective adopters home situations as he'd done for PARRT. Stepped visits to slowly introduce adopter and adopted resulted in less cases of rejection, which reduced the animals' chances of finding permanent homes as they grew older. He enjoyed the work, though menial, and although the staff situation continued to be quite threatening, his dedication and refusal to quit eventually won him some begrudged respect.

After a few months a German Shepherd, Sasha, was brought in by the RSPCA. She was the subject of an ongoing prosecution alleging cruelty by her owner, and was in very poor condition, rating only 1 out of 9 by the examining vet. Because she'd never been exercised the muscles in her back legs had atrophied completely meaning she couldn't stand properly; she was extremely thin and mange had stripped most of her fur. As part of her recovery treatment she was booked for a course of hydrotherapy and because Stephen showed interest in the bedraggled, unattractive urchin and volunteered the use of his own vehicle, he was allowed the task of taking her there and back.

He was very impressed by the skills and knowledge of Trevor, who ran 4Paws at Whitehouse Farm on the outskirts of Morpeth, as he watched Sasha steadily improve in both health and temperament. He was used to dogs being kept locked in cages with minimal exercise, but now he paid close attention and learned about muscle wastage, strength, stamina, and caring for joints, tendons and ligaments. His interest in German Shepherds continued through Sasha and particularly their inherent physical problems such as the dying of nerve cells during degenerative myelopathy (DM).

Sasha's limbs strengthened rapidly over the next few months and her skin improved visibly with medicinal baths. The muscles in her legs recovered and she was able to stand properly, so consequently could exercise more and was much happier. All this was very positive and much different from what happened at Weston Vale - where animals were simply shunted through the system as fast as possible with little thought given to their overall, ongoing health.

One facet that did worry Stephen, was that even when an animal is removed from an owner who has already been banned from keeping them previously, that animal still has to be penned up for months and sometimes years, until the resultant litigation ends.

'So if an owner's already been banned from keeping any animals, none can be returned to him can they?' Stephen asked Gerry, one of the RSPCA inspectors who checked in on Sasha regularly.

'No, obviously not, at least not during the ban period.'

'So what's the point of keeping the latest confiscated animal in kennels instead of re-homing it as soon as possible?'

'It's because the animal itself is evidence in the case, so must be preserved as such.'

'But the courts accept photographic and video evidence don't they?'

'Yes but if the owner wins the case he can claim his animal back.'

'But not if he's already banned from keeping an animal?'

'Mm, see where you're coming from, but that's the way the law is and we have to abide by it.'

Shortly after this conversation Stephen was called to one side by Tracy, who admonished him for 'bothering' the RSPCA inspectors. 'They haven't time to be talking to you for hours on end,' she said. 'And you certainly haven't the time to be pestering them.'

Stephen was afraid of losing his new access to the RSPCA kennels, which he found the most interesting, so quickly apologised.

'Well just remember in future - don't interfere with the RSPCA staff and if there's ever anything we need to talk to them about - I'll be doing it.'

He felt as if he was swimming for a very distant shore but slowly drowning in the attempt.

Seventeen

KYLE

Another German Shepherd, Kyle, came in suffering from mange and although the infection was brought under control quite quickly, his fur never grew back completely because the hair follicles were so badly damaged by flea infestation during years of neglect. His skin was very sensitive and Stephen was given the job of lathering him up and washing him in a weekly medicated bath. He was very careful because of the dog's tender skin, and Kyle slowly learned to trust him. The relevant RSPCA inspector came in regularly to check on the dog's progress, and Stephen asked about different problems and treatments related to the breed.

He spent a lot of time with Kyle, who was listed as aggressive, but Stephen got to know him better than anybody, walked him with other dogs and knew that he only displayed aggression defensively when his skin was aggravated. The RSPCA staff were amazed at Kyle's progress and the change in his behaviour, and knew that it had been achieved by Stephen's dedicated time and effort. Eventually the case went to court and the owner convicted, fined and banned from keeping animals yet again. The successful prosecution was reported in the local press with a picture of Kyle and the East Meadow girls. Now the case was over, Gerry asked Stephen personally if he could re-home the dog.

'I'll give it my best shot,' he replied.

'There's a problem though.'

'Yeah?'

'Yes, we've only got one week's budget left for him now the legals are over and costs awarded.'

'Shit, that's no time at all but I'll tell you what - if I can't re-home him straight off I'll put him in one of the private kennels until I can.'

'Yeah, how's that work?'

'Well, I've already got two of my own rescues in there at a fiver a day, so I'll just rent another until I find a home for him.'

'At your own expense?'

'Yup.'

'Okay, if you're sure you're willing to do that for him?'

'Of course I am - he's my pal now and the alternative's killing him - and no way does he deserve that.'

The feeling of saving the misunderstood dog was very gratifying, and as a double fallback Stephen spoke to Helen at Hamsterley Hall, who reassured him that she would find temporary room for Kyle if necessary. Two hours later Gerry telephoned to say the deal was off.

'What, why?'

'We've had discussions with your management and they say the dog's too dangerous to be given another chance.'

'You mean Tracy?'

Gerry didn't answer.

'Gerry, Tracy has no qualifications whatsoever to make a decision like that.'

'Well she's told us she has more experience than you with problem dogs, and she's in a more senior position so we have no option but to accept her opinion.'

'Has this got something to do with the discount you get here, Gerry?'

A few seconds silence followed and then the line went dead. Stephen went to confront Tracy, who was expecting him and launched into a tirade about following instructions, doing what he was told and not questioning her management decisions. He realised that Kyle was lost and considered just putting him in the car and taking off, but knew the first thing Tracy would do with immense satisfaction was call the police.

'So when's the vet coming?' he asked dejectedly.

'He's not.'

'He's not?'

'No, it's my professional opinion that this dog that you've wasted so much of our time on, is too dangerous for our normal procedure.'

'So, so what's going to happen to him?'

'He'll be taken out into the yard and shot in the back of the head when he's not looking.'

'Shot in the head - are you fucking serious?'

'I'm perfectly serious and don't you dare speak to me like that or I'll have you removed from site.'

'Is that even legal - shooting a dog who isn't a threat to anyone or anything?'

'Of course it's legal, it'll be carried out by a qualified officer who has the authority to do so.'

'Tracy, even the police can be prosecuted for shooting a person or an animal without just cause, and the RSPCA themselves have been investigated for shooting dogs in the past.'

'I've had quite enough of your insolence and troublemaking Stephen, and I warn you now that if you don't remove yourself from this office immediately, you'll be removed forcibly.'

'When's it happening?' he croaked, wiping tears from his face as he realised further resistance was futile.

'Tomorrow morning and stop being so soft, you shouldn't get so emotionally involved - it's unprofessional. Now if you'll excuse me I have work to do.'

Stephen didn't sleep that night and the following day kept busy cleaning kennels with a weary heart, and was not allowed any access to Kyle. At about 10.30 he heard a vehicle pull up on the gravel and looked outside to see a white van with blue logo on the side. A man wearing a coverall suit got out and walked towards the office carrying something under his arm.

Stephen grabbed a lead from its hook on the wall, and quickly took one of the dogs out in the opposite direction. He walked quickly without looking back, but didn't get too far into the distance before hearing a loud bang, which he knew without doubt was a gunshot. But not from an ordinary gun - it was a captive bolt-gun as also used in slaughterhouses to kill animals cheaply before butchery.

He sat down and rested against a wall until the strength returned to his legs, then walked back slowly, re-penned the dog and went home.

Next day he got up, told himself he had to be professional, and went back to work. He carried on as normal; cleaning, feeding and dog-walking, and as he got thirty yards along the rear path, came across a large patch of bloodstained ground. Nobody had even bothered to clean up after the unwarranted execution, despite Stephen being told later that Tracy was actively involved in it. He was also told that the kill wasn't clean and that no vet was present. No part of this gruesome follow-up to Kyle's success in court, was ever reported in the press.

After Stephen made his views known in no uncertain terms again, he was effectively a dead man walking as far as his future at East Meadow was concerned. He was restricted to the dirtiest cleaning jobs with no animal contact but even so, an avalanche of absurd complaints by staff members were recorded by Tracy against him. When he asked for evidence in support of any of the complaints, none was forthcoming.

Stephen was approached by a young man called Gregg, who was studying for a university degree in Canine Psychology and wanted to accrue as much practical experience as possible. He'd seen Stephen's successes online and also wanted to work with troubled, rescued dogs. Appreciating his good intentions, Stephen sidestepped Tracy to ask Lucy if Gregg could help out with the dogs he was paying for to be kennelled. Lucy agreed and the lad proved to be very knowledgeable, which came to the notice of the RSPCA staff who sought his opinion on various issues. This inevitably annoyed Tracy and her gang, which made the situation even worse for Stephen when they discovered Gregg was there at his secret request. One positive outcome however, was that because of Gregg's input, Stephen's online profile soared to new heights which additionally irritated Tracy's jealousy.

A white, English Bull Terrier with a skin condition was brought in by the RSPCA and Stephen was asked by Gerry to help re-home it.

'No, I won't *help* re-home him,' he replied, recalling recent horrific events. 'But what I will do is re-home him myself, either here with my other rescues, or at another shelter until I've assessed him for the treatment he needs.'

'Yeah okay, I think we can go with that,' said Gerry.

104

'Okay, leave him in the empty pen over there until I finish cleaning, then I'll sort the situation out.'

Stephen went off to finish his last task of the day, which was scraping and washing out the pigsty. He completed it as fast as possible and rushed back, to find the pen empty. Tracy had found out what was going on behind her back, as she chose to see it, called the vet and had the poor dog put to sleep immediately.

Both Stephen and Gregg were appalled and wondered just what kind of monsters they were working with. There and then they made the decision to leave and as donations to Shak were increasing considerably, they registered it officially with the Charity Commission, naming Gregg as co-Trustee. Although Stephen could have claimed compensation through an industrial tribunal for Constructive Dismissal and Discrimination from East Meadow, he decided against it because he didn't want to deprive Lucy's business of much needed funds to the point of probable financial collapse.

'So what will you do now?' asked Gregg.

'Well, the first thing I'm going to do is use the month's wages to take my family on holiday for a week.'

'Lucky you.'

'Yeah but they haven't had a real break for a long time, and they definitely need one after all the crap I've been taking home with me over the past two years.'

A while later Stephen bumped into Lucy in Morrisons car park at Alnwick, where she praised him for his determination and charity work, and lamented the suffering he'd endured at East Meadow.

Eighteen

UNCERTAINTY

Elaine and Stephen agreed on a week at a small resort just north of Barcelona and despite their new worries about the future, enjoyed having free time in the sunshine with Neve.

'So where do we go from here?' Elaine asked her husband as their daughter played in the sand, oblivious to the problems that were never allowed to affect her life.

'I'm not sure,' he admitted.

'You must feel better though, now you're away from that horrible place at last?'

'Well I'm certainly more relaxed at the moment,' he smiled, tilting up his sunglasses and sipping a cold beer. 'Massively relieved in fact but also a little lost - I've just walked out of my third job in two years which must be worrying for you? I was a reasonably normal, successful bloke with a steady income when we met.'

'I understand you not wanting to be somewhere you're not happy.'

'I know you do Elaine and I'm grateful, but we have a daughter to provide for and a home to maintain, and I've got a growing number of dogs to look after.'

'So what will you do?'

'Well, I was already trawling the papers back home and I've just found an internet café in the village here, so for now I'll see if I can find something in the phone industry.'

'Are you sure, I didn't think you'd ever go back to that?'

'I'm just thinking short-term for now, until we get back on our feet and see how the land lies, you know?'

'So you won't be talking to your old partner, David?'

'No, it wouldn't be fair on him and I don't want to get involved to that extent again anyway.'

All he could find were call-centre jobs so registered with half a dozen, and when the family returned from holiday he found two replies waiting in his inbox. Both were from industry giant, Orange - one for a position in Darlington and the other at the Cobalt centre near North Shields, just west of the Tyne estuary on the north bank. They invited him for interview and he accepted, attended and was offered two positions from which he chose the most senior - as a Platinum Business-Customer Services Adviser at North Shields. The advice he gave was totally by and about telephones over three 12-hour shifts, plus a half-day at weekends. The hours were attractive because they left time for him to continue his rescue work.

He settled in quickly and his talents were soon spotted by Team Manager, Sharon who used him as a stand-in for herself during busy periods and holidays. Stephen calculated that there might well be a good chance of promotion in the future and his optimism rose along with the boost to his self-confidence. It was work he'd grown weary of long ago, but was obviously very good at and the break from it had restored some enthusiasm.

Elaine had been worried about the future during her husband's unpleasant period at East Meadow, but fully understood his position and supported him in it. She noted his more positive attitude now though and despite knowing he would never give up his vision to save more dogs or weaken in his resolve to change the cruelty of current systems, she appreciated the release of tension and pervading gloom from the household.

The lift in Elaine's spirits had a reciprocally positive effect on Stephen, who allowed the thought to enter his mind that he should concentrate on the new job and his family, and their joint, long-term prospects. But Shak was now a registered charity, gaining interest and momentum, and he knew without doubt that if he let it all go now he'd regret it for the rest of his life. He knew that one day in the future he could be sitting pretty in an upgraded home, picking out his next new car and foreign holiday, but eventually he'd come across something that would interrupt his self-satisfaction by reminding him of all the horrific cruelty to animals across the world, and hate himself for giving up the opportunity to do something about it, in a way he'd already worked so hard and sacrificed so much to create. He'd look around at all his expensive luxuries and wonder, apart from his wife and daughter and the pets he kept at home, what exactly had been the point of his life – simply to increase use of the mobile telephone and make himself richer? That would never be enough.

So for now he'd continue with both occupations and although it stretched his time and energy to the limit, other people appreciated his efforts. His mother had recently retired and noticing how much pressure he was under during his days off from Orange, asked, 'Is there anything I can do to help?'

'Not really,' he answered, holding his phone whilst trying to locate a pen under a pile of paperwork on the kitchen table, so he could take notes from the caller.

'Well I could answer the phone so you could find your pen,' she replied with a smile.

He looked at her.

'In fact I could probably take notes as well so you could do something more important.'

She took over there and then, later included organising and running fund-raising events, and was often joined by Elaine in her spare time. The additional income paid kennelling fees for the rescued dogs as their number increased to eight, but the increase took up even more of Stephen's already stretched time, as he had to personally take charge of modifying the animals' behaviour and health to the point of re-homeability.

His employment with Orange also intensified as Sharon relied on him more and more, and he began to think seriously about applying for a more senior position in the hope that it would allow him to delegate some of his most time-consuming duties. Official promotion continued to evade him because he was so useful at his present level, but he was asked to take on increasingly demanding responsibilities including floor-walking, to help colleagues with problem customers as they occurred, also assisting with technical data particularly regarding the newly released Blackberry phones, and eventually with training staff in general duties. He even set up a computer programme to assist training and leave more time to take escalated calls from customers who were overly irate and couldn't be pacified by the initial responder.

Soon he worked almost exclusively in management roles and although he wasn't paid at that level, he enjoyed the work and was reasonably content with his salary. His working relationship with Sharon intensified which made both their jobs easier, and on several occasions he found himself laughing with her and other colleagues about various situations. He rediscovered the sense of humour he'd lost watching dogs being put to death, felt much better for it and again, Elaine was encouraged by the fact that it derived from a return to the type of work he'd previously rejected but was so successful at.

Eventually and inevitably though, he became despondent over several months at not being offered promotion, and felt that he was simply being used by the company without due reward. As the novelty of his new tasks wore off, the dream and ambition of running his own dog sanctuary returned to prominence in his mind. He mentioned it to Sharon who asked him, 'You must really hate this job then, do you?'

'I like working with you Sharon and you've helped me a lot. I just hate having to sort out other peoples' problems all the time and not being paid the going rate for it.'

'Not the best situation is it?'

'Not really but I know it's not your fault.'

'So you'll be leaving me eventually, one way or the other?'

'Looks that way I'm afraid.'

Nineteen

MISS BLUE SKY

Stephen carried on working for Orange as Shak continued to grow, as did Neve who was now three years old. Poppy came to the end of her life after fifteen years; most of them as part of Stephen's family and therefore good ones. Whilst quaffing a couple of pints in her memory at the weekend, he was told about a racing Greyhound which had been retired because of an injury, and was now going to be used as a constantly-caged breeding machine by its callous owner.

The once-successful racer which had worked hard over many years, was being kept in private kennel space rented on a farm at West Horton, whilst recovering from a leg injury. The more Stephen thought about the fate that awaited the dog - the more determined he became to do something about it. The following day he drove up to the farm and spoke to Doreen, who ran the kennels.

'I totally agree,' she said after Stephen broached the subject of the unfortunate Greyhound. 'It's such a shame especially after she won so many races for him, but they don't care about that, they're only interested in the money side of things.'

'What's the bloke like?'

'He's a stubborn old buggar but you'll be able to judge for yourself in a minute,' she answered, turning to watch a white van crunch across the gravel into the yard.

'How's she doing then?' the driver asked as he got out of the cab, nodding at Stephen but otherwise ignoring him.

'She's on the mend,' Doreen replied, leading him into the kennels building.

Stephen followed across bare earth until they stopped to look at a white Greyhound with grey patches, limping around a cage with one leg strapped up.

'At least she can stand up on her own now,' Doreen said.

The dog stayed at the far side of the cage, staring fearfully at them and making no move towards its owner.

'Aye, she'll be no good for racing anymore but I'll get a good few pups out of her to sell,' he laughed.

Stephen felt his anger rise but said calmly, 'So what's she worth now then?'

The owner looked at Stephen as if for the first time, probably thinking he was a kennel worker or volunteer, and replied, 'Well look at her - not a lot that's for sure. She's been a canny bitch and won me a few quid in the past, but I doubt I'd get fifty for her now.'

Stephen looked at the sad, injured dog tottering on three legs and said, 'I'll give you fifty for her.'

The owner laughed and puffed on his cigarette.

'I'm serious.'

He looked round again, blowing smoke in Stephen's face as he asked, 'You got the fifty on you now, then?'

'Uh-hum.'

Stephen bought the Greyhound there and then, took her home and bathed her, and named her Sky because her racing name was Miss Blue Sky. He kept her at home where he put his recovery skills to good use, never sent her to kennels and kept in touch with Doreen after she telephoned to ask how the dog was doing. At the end of one conversation she added, 'Oh by the way, just in case you were planning to visit us again in the future, we've made an offer for a place near Hexham so we can live on site, so we'll most likely be moving.'

'Oh, right.'

'Yes, it has accommodation so will save us having to rent a house, and looks like it might well go ahead quite soon.'

'Oh well, best of luck and if you do move and the West Horton place is vacant, give me a call,' he laughed.

The next time he got a call from Doreen he was busy with a particularly difficult customer at work, so let it go to voicemail. He checked later, saw it was from her and put off answering until he'd dealt with the next telephone crisis, but then received a text message. While still talking to a client he pulled his phone out and read: 'Please call me as soon as you can - Doreen.'

Not another injured, undervalued dog, he hoped as he returned her call during his lunch break.

'Oh Stephen,' she answered. 'I'm so glad you got back to me.'

'Hi Doreen, another problem?' he asked.

'No, no I just wanted to let you know that the deal has gone through and we're leaving West Horton.'

'Oh, right, congratulations.'

'Thank you. Yes, we got the place at Hexham and have given George the farmer a month's notice, and I told him about you.'

'Oh, did you?'

'Yes, you were serious about taking the place on, weren't you?'

'Oh er, yes of course, so what did he say?'

'He said he'll talk to you about it if you go up to see him.'

The news hit like a bolt of lightning which lit up the path in front of him, and although he hadn't the slightest clue as to how he could pay the rent on such a big place, he called the farmer and arranged a meeting for his next day off work.

Twenty

HOME

'Hello there, my name's George,' said the West Horton farmer when he met Stephen outside the kennels.

'I'm Stephen and I'm pleased to meet you George,' Stephen replied, shaking hands.

'Doreen tells me you're interested in taking the place on?'

'I might be, but it kind of depends on the rent and suchlike.'

'Well, I'm sure we can reach an agreement on the rent if we're talking long-term and you're taking over as soon as Doreen leaves, but there's something we have to sort out first.'

'Oh right, what's that then?'

'It's these dangerous dogs you're planning to bring up here, because this is still a working farm you understand. I've got other animals here that can't be put in danger.'

'Who said I was bringing dangerous dogs?'

'Well…well…'

'It doesn't matter George. Look, they're not dangerous - they're abused dogs and they're nervous because they've been badly treated in the past, sometimes for years and if I don't save them, nobody will and they'll be put to sleep.'

George looked at him with a strange grimace on his face.

'Have you any idea how many innocent dogs are killed just because stupid people throw them out on the street and there's no room to keep them anywhere?'

George shook his head.

'Thousands, tens of thousands every bloody year and it's not because they're dangerous - it's because nobody will give them kennel space or take a minute to understand what's going on in their heads after all the shite they've been put through!'

George continued to stare at him in silence as if watching a lunatic.

'And we're very competent handlers as well - we know exactly what we're doing and my partner Gregg's bringing new techniques in from his university course all the time.'

'University course? George asked tentatively.

'Yes, he's studying for a degree in Canine Psychology by distance-learning as well as working full time and volunteering with me. He learns about body-language, calming-signals, behavioural patterns and how to set up scenarios to assess and treat problems, and he passes it all on to me. '

118

'Right...well...I'll need time to think about it obviously. I've got your number so I'll call you.'

'Okay, thanks for your time anyway,' Stephen replied, certain that he'd blown it and no way would George call him.

But two days later he did to say, 'Right Stephen, I've thought things over and I'm prepared to give it a go, but on the strict understanding that none of my sheep will come to any harm, and if they do - you'll be responsible for full financial restitution.'

'I'll agree to that George, and thank you on behalf of all the extra dogs we can help now.'

As Shak's online profile grew he was repeatedly contacted by shelters and rescue centres which didn't have the facilities, expertise or inclination to care for dogs labelled problematic, asking if he could take them in. He knew that such establishments charged either the RSPCA or other rescue organisations for the space and time, and now he had 32 pens of his own. After discussions with Gregg who was still increasing online interest in Shak from the general public, they agreed to immediately take in the most critical cases to kennel capacity, arrange to switch payments from the releasing shelter to Shak, and also look into expanding their available space.

'Then we can go nationwide,' said Gregg eagerly.

'Yeah but make sure it's clear that we are not a temporary dumping ground for unwanted animals - we're a permanent sanctuary for condemned dogs on death-row, wherever that might be - and we guarantee a safe home and kind treatment for the rest of their lives. They'll get care, exercise, behavioural and medical treatment and we will never kill an animal unless it's to prevent that animal suffering.'

Things did not go as smoothly as hoped though, when Doreen's moving plans drifted astray. A problem with the Hexham property documentation prevented her and her husband moving out of West Horton, which in turn prevented Shak moving in. Stephen had been trying to coincide the move with the expiration of his notice to Orange, so he'd have money coming in for as long as possible until up and running with the charity, though he hadn't really planned in any detail beyond that.

Another related problem which arose was that the shelters only wanted to pay for kennelling at Shak for the shortest possible period, and during negotiations demanded that each dog must be processed and ready for re-homing within the first month.

'No, I'm afraid we don't do that,' Stephen tried to explain to a particularly difficult client.

'What do you mean, you don't do that?' he demanded.

'We don't do re-homing, we haven't time to carry out home-checks on applicants and all the rest of it - we save lives and treat problems and…'

'I'm not bothered about home-checks and treatments, I just want their behaviour modified so they're ready to go within a month at the most - I can't afford to keep paying you forever.'

'Alright look, you should be bothered and I'm not interested in how much money you've got, and I cannot guarantee that any dog will be ready to move on in a month or a year or ever. I'm only concerned with the dogs' welfare so just pay for the first month and I'll take it from there.'

'Oh er, that sounds reasonable I suppose, alright we'll agree on that.'

Things began to move very quickly which left Stephen with a stark choice: either he accepted the dogs in need that came to him now, trusting to luck that he'd be in West Horton before total overload occurred, or he rejected them and crippled Shak before it even got up on its feet? He chose the former without much deliberation and handed in a month's notice to Sharon, who was disappointed but not surprised, and ultimately pleased for Stephen and his new venture.

He stuck it out for the month during which time he thought long and hard about his future financial position, and discovering that the Charity Commission had a financial adviser, telephoned one lunch-time.

'Well the first thing to make absolutely clear,' said Raymond the adviser. 'Is that you cannot take a wage or salary as Trustee of a registered charity at this point.'

'No, I thought not.'

'But...'

'Uh-hum?'

'You could be paid for providing a professional service to the charity.'

'A professional service?'

'Yes.'

'So how does that work?'

'Well, as I understand your position, your organisation rescues and treats dogs in dire need?'

'Yes, that's what we do.'

'And at the moment you pay other kennels to house the rescued dogs, is that correct?'

'Yes that's what we've been doing up to now but I'm waiting to take over kennels myself.'

'Right, so just back up a step: the kennels that you currently pay to house the dogs are - providing you with a professional service.'

'Are they? Oh yes, of course they are.'

'So you see, when you move the dogs to your new kennels, you in fact will be…'

'Providing Shak with a professional service?'

'Exactly.'

'I see…'

'And of course, although you're not setting out as a profit-making enterprise, you could quite legitimately do what many other kennelling providers do, which is split your space into part rescue and part private hire; charging the usual commercial rates for the latter, to subsidise the former.'

'I see, that would be great at least until we're up and running and still have some spare room.'

'Precisely, and if privately-acquired funds can be used, you are actually using your own money to help create a worthy charity, so it doesn't have to rely solely on donations and external funding - which is all to the good.'

'I think it could work, Raymond.'

'I'm quite certain it would work, Mr Wylie.'

'Well thank you for your advice.'

Twenty One

MONA

The number of dogs Shak was caring for increased over the weeks to sixteen, all kennelled privately and Stephen had cancelled their tenure from the date he originally expected to move into West Horton, which wasn't vacant on that date. He kept calm, phoned around and found them all temporary lodgings at Embleton, again at private rates, but knew he couldn't finance that move for very long.

As winter approached his notice at work ran out and he said goodbye to his colleagues at Orange, who knew he'd be spending much of his time outdoors or in big open spaces, so had all chipped in to buy him a selection of thermal underwear. Despite missing the traditional bottle of spirits he was grateful eventually, and wore them to care for his dogs after the thirty miles or so drive from Bedlington onto the A1, the B1340 and 1339 to Embleton every day, and then back again for week after week as his financial concerns grew. Elaine and his mother also had grave worries and wondered if Stephen had finally made a disastrous mistake by leaving his job and future prospects behind, and instead committing to an as-yet unavailable home for Shak. Stephen himself admitted he'd been lucky to land the job with Orange so close to home, but could he ever be as lucky again? Small worries and concerns if left unchecked for long periods - can have big consequences, they all knew.

Eventually Stephen received the go-ahead and on Friday 11th September 2009, moved into West Horton to set up the Shak sanctuary. Gregg was very busy with his clerical, government job in the Regent Centre, Gosforth so Stephen loaded, transported, unloaded and settled all the dogs on his own, plus all the equipment they'd collected over the preceding three years. It was a tiring but immensely satisfying day and he knew that at long last, Shak was going to be a reality in its own right. As if to confirm that fact, at the end of the day Stephen received a call from Jenny who worked at a shelter in Birmingham, pleading with him to take in a female Staffordshire Bull Terrier which was due to be killed two days later on Monday morning.

'It's late in the day and I'm exhausted Jenny,' he replied. 'Can you get her here?'

'I'm on my way,' she answered. 'Text me your new postcode?'

Mona the Staffie was the first new entrant directly to Shak's official home, and soon undergoing lengthy treatment to modify her nervous and unsociable behaviour.

On Saturday Stephen got out of bed early to cut the grass at home before going to work. It was a warm, dry day and might be his last chance before winter kicked in - the weather can be very unpredictable in north Northumberland, which in ancient times stretched as far south as the River Humber, from where the name derives: north of the Humber land.

He hadn't yet had time to set up an office at the farm so checked his emails before leaving, and found one from Jenny. It thanked him for saving Mona but also had an attached list of dogs with a photograph of each. He glanced through them while sipping a black coffee after stowing the mower away, and noticed a German Shepherd which looked odd. He was still always attracted to the breed and taking another look before switching the laptop off, decided it must have something wrong with its left eye. He got in the truck and headed off, immediately appreciating the vast, open countryside around him, but his thoughts kept wandering back to the Shepherd with the injured eye. It bothered him all way until he parked up at West Horton and pulled out his phone.

'What's the story on Scooby the Shepherd?' he asked Jenny, who was still at home eating breakfast.

'Oh right - the list I sent out; I should've taken him off because he's been moved to a different list for Monday, unfortunately.'

'The kill-list?'

'Afraid so, we just can't get anywhere near him. His cage hasn't been cleaned since he arrived because he won't let anybody in.'

'What happened to his eye?'

'You don't want to know, Stephen,' she replied, crunching a mouthful of low-sugar muesli.

'I do want to know, Jenny.'

'Alright,' she said, putting down her spoon. 'His owners did a midnight-flit owing rent, and left him chained to a tree in the back garden for God knows how long.'

'The bastards.'

'The dog-warden was eventually called out but couldn't even get into the garden with him, and one of the neighbours looked over the fence to tell him the dog was called Scooby, and was blind in one eye because its owner had stabbed him with a screwdriver.'

'Jesus Christ and you wonder why he's aggressive and defensive?'

'Unfortunately the underlying reasons don't count for much now.'

At that precise point, knowing Jenny's words were so true, Stephen realised that Scooby was a perfect example of what Shak stood for and why he'd created it, and without considering the details any further said, 'I'll take him.'

'Oh no I'm sorry Stephen, he's way too big and aggressive and he's already eight years old, so we just cannot pass him on to anybody else and anyway - it's too late for him now.'

'It was almost too late for Mona yesterday.'

'That's a whole different case though - she's withdrawn but not vicious like Scooby.'

'So he's on the list for the same vet visit?'

'Uh-hum, Monday morning and today's Saturday.'

'Alright Jenny now listen - I already know how this dog's mind is working. He's probably been beaten and abused all his life and just doesn't trust people for a second.'

'You're definitely right there.'

'But I can get to him - I've been studying behaviour in Shepherds, and I can sort him out to the point where he can at least spend the rest of his life in peace and comfort.'

'I hear what you're saying Stephen but we just can't let him go - we'd be making ourselves liable if anything happened - and I'm pretty sure something would.'

'I'll sign a full disclaimer relieving you and your organisation and the local authority of all responsibility, and give it to you before I collect him.'

'You'd come to collect him?'

'Yes, definitely, I couldn't ask you to drive all the way up here again so soon.'

Jenny paused and Stephen could hear her spoon clink against the breakfast bowl. He waited.

'Okay I'll tell you what,' she finally said. 'No way am I convinced that this will work but because it's you and you're a competent and experienced handler, and because you took Mona in for me - I'll have a word with the head warden.'

'When?'

'Well, it'll be Monday now.'

'Monday will be too late, Jen.'

She paused again. 'Alright look, I'll try his mobile but I cannot guarantee that he'll answer, particularly on a Saturday.'

'Thank you Jen.'

'How is Mona by the way?'

'She's absolutely fine.'

'Okay, I'll get back to you if I have any luck.'

Twenty Two

SCOOBY

T he day dragged by with no return call from Birmingham. Stephen finished work and went home and to keep his mind occupied whilst Elaine prepared their evening meal, he began pulling weeds and pruning plants around the neatly-mown lawn. It had been another warm, sunny day with some scattered cloud and in the east he could see a low fog-bank, or fret in local parlance, rolling in from the North Sea. Neve came out into the garden with two dogs and he asked her, 'Is tea ready yet?'

'It won't be long, dad,' she replied before running off to play with the dogs.

'Well,' he said, watching them chase each other around in a circle as he stuck the shears point down in the grass. 'Doesn't look like I'm going to get the call I've been waiting for and there's nothing else I can do, so I think I'll try a cold beer or two before we eat.'

Neve lay on the grass next to her father who was halfway through a second bottle of lager, when his mobile buzzed. He fumbled it out of his pocket, dropped it on the lawn, picked it up with a fistful of grass cuttings and pushed the green button. The phone was dead. He checked the caller number and rang it.

'Hello?' a male voice answered.

'Oh, hello,' Stephen said, half expecting to hear Jenny. 'Did you just call me?'

'Is that Mr Wylie?'

'Yes, yes it is.'

'Hello Mr Wylie, this is Maurice, I'm head dog-warden for the Birmingham area. I've received a request to speak to you about a certain dog at the Walsall shelter.'

'Oh right, yes, and thank you for taking the time to call on Saturday.'

'That's alright but look, you must realise just how dangerous this particular dog is, and that he certainly cannot be re-homed?'

'Yes, I do realise that, I've discussed it all with the shelter staff and I have no intention of re-homing him.'

'Oh, well now you've confused me - so what exactly do you intend to do with him?'

'I've started a whole new venture - a sort of retirement home for dogs that've had a rough time of it and have nowhere else to go. We take them in, give them a home for life and look after them properly.'

'Mm, you sound like you're on a bit of a mission?'

'You could say that - we're just very determined to save dogs which don't deserve to die, and as Jenny at the shelter will tell you, we know what we're doing and have been very successful so far.'

'Yes, Jenny does sing your praises somewhat, that's actually why I made this call.'

'So can we have the dog?'

'Well, I suppose you can try but you'll have to collect him, I definitely cannot allow any staff in my area to even attempt to handle him.'

'That's fine, I'm more than happy to come down for him.'

'And you will definitely have to sign our disclaimer, releasing us from all responsibility once he's moved from our shelter.'

'No problem Maurice, I'll sign it as soon as I get there.'

'And when will that be?'

'It'll be tomorrow morning. I definitely don't want him at the shelter when the vet comes around on Monday.'

'Alright, well I won't be there tomorrow but the best of luck to you.'

'Thank you again.'

At 5.30am next day Stephen took Oskar and Sky for their morning walk along the River Blyth at the bottom of Furnace Bank, and as they went through the gravelled parking area he noticed a glass jar standing on an upright boundary stone. Glancing inside he saw a number of Stickleback fish, apparently left to die in the heat of the coming day as no-one was around. He continued past but then stopped, remembering that fish are also living

131

creatures which feel pain and discomfort, so backtracked, picked up the jar and emptied the little Sticklebacks back into the river from where they'd obviously been taken. He smiled as they swam away in the cool, clear water, free again against the odds, and carried on along the south bank.

Later that morning when he reached the Walsall shelter, word was obviously out that a northern lunatic was coming down, as a number of staff members were already clustered around Scooby's cage. The dog was barking loudly in obvious warning not to approach further, which was apparently his normal behaviour if anybody came within five yards of him.

Stephen asked the audience to leave and sat on the ground outside the bars, talking softly to the nervous animal. After twenty minutes it had calmed down enough to accept some hot-dog sausage - a culinary tip learned from Gregg, and quarter of an hour later Stephen eased open the gate. He kept feeding the dog as he deftly looped a slip-lead over its head, and making sure nobody was within striking distance outside, slowly led it from the cage, through the shelter and onto a grassed area at the rear. Staff watched in amazement as the pair walked around calmly for half an hour, and then made their way to the back of Stephen's Mitsubishi Warrior.

He dropped the tailgate, lifted the screen and Scooby was happy to jump in, but didn't quite make it and without pausing to think, Stephen put his hands under the dog's rear end to help it up. It whipped around in defence and clamped its teeth into his left forearm. Blood started to flow immediately but at least Scooby let go straight away. Hoping the past two hours hadn't been wasted by his mistake, he asked the staff who were still standing around watching to hold the lead while he patched his arm, but they refused saying they weren't allowed to. They did though, bring a bowl of water for the dog which was panting, probably because of anxiety, and as Stephen moved around to re-position himself for another attempt at loading the dog into the truck, he realised too late that he'd approached on its blind side and again panicked it, and this time it bit into his calf.

He looked down at his bloody injuries and smiled at the silent shelter staff saying, 'Jenny did tell you I was an expert at this stuff didn't she?'

They weren't amused but one did say, 'We've called her to come over but she hasn't answered yet. Probably had a late night out 'cause it's her day off today.'

Scooby lay on the gravel, growling and snarling at every movement in a stand-off that lasted almost four hours. Eventually Jenny showed up with a colleague called John and dragged a large cage out into the yard. John linked another lead to the one Stephen was still holding, to double its length, then threaded it through the cage and out of the bars at the back. Jenny brought a bowl of rich-aroma food out and placed it in the cage, and stood well back. Scooby caught the scent and went straight into the cage as John tightened his lead from the back, so he couldn't retreat, and Stephen clicked the gate shut behind him.

Jenny then brought two yard-brooms which she poked between the horizontal bars to either side of the cage, and now the dog was contained other staff members came forward to grasp the broom handles at all four corners, and lift the cage into the truck.

Stephen quickly washed and patched his wounds, thanked all the staff for their assistance, gave Jenny and John a grateful hug and set off home. After an hour when he thought the dog might have settled, he stopped at a filling-station and opened the back of the truck to let some fresh air in. A low growl slowly built up in the darkness so he shut it again and carried on driving. Eventually he got Scooby back to West Horton and into a kennel by pushing the crate up to its open door and placing some food inside. He then went to hospital to get his lacerations stitched up, but not even Gregg could get close enough to the dog to get the double lead off.

On his release from hospital Stephen poked a litter-picker through the bars of Scooby's cage, grabbed the end of the lead and was able to take him out for a walk on a rigid leash while still keeping his distance. For at least an hour every day he sat on the ground outside the cage, never on Scooby's left side and never touching him; just talking softly and feeding him treats. In time they became good friends; the dog showed no aggression at all and behaved just like a pet. After a few months of ongoing therapy, Stephen was even able to use him as a calming influence on other dogs.

Scooby's successful transformation was a glowing report on Shak's worth and ethos. Gregg made certain that a photographic record of his progress was prominently posted online for all to see, and they soon sold out of hastily printed Scooby Fan Club tee-shirts. Stephen was proved right in his beliefs and after a shaky start, rose to celebrity status in the Birmingham area's animal welfare community, particularly after being savaged by the dog in question but not giving up on it!

Not long afterwards Shak was approached by Northumberland County Council's Head of Animal Welfare, and asked to provide a collection service for animals reported as strays outside normal business hours. The service wasn't to be comprehensive as it would only run from 5pm to 11pm, but the council thereby fulfilled its obligation to provide a suitable place for members of the public to deposit strays. The financial recompense wasn't great but very welcome, and rescuing animals from the streets was a worthy cause so Stephen accepted.

After expecting a deluge of calls he was surprised to receive not even one for two weeks, but waited muzzle-in-hand by the phone every evening so he wouldn't be late for the first. He finally got it at 6.34pm one Saturday. A local girl had found an apparent stray on Cambois Beach, off the A189 between Blyth and Newbiggin-by-the-Sea, where ex-England footballer and 1966 World Cup winner Jack Charlton's son, John, runs his dog-friendly pub and serves extremely good-value meals which include the best home-made chips for miles around!

The girl took the dog home and Stephen attended her house, close to the small, private boat-yard looking east across the Wansbeck estuary, to find the young dog in excellent condition and micro-chipped. Stephen was trained and authorised to retrieve stored identification information, and discovered that the dog was registered to a nearby address, slightly further inland. It was only a short walk away so he thanked the girl for helping the dog, put it on leash and set off. The dog started pulling straight away and obviously knew its way home, so Stephen was happy for it to lead him there.

'So all's well that ends well,' he said to himself with a smile as he drove back home to await the next callout.

Gregg had promised to share them which would lighten the load, and Shak was now a recognised charity with an excellent reputation. So all was set for the future?

Twenty Three

NO WAY BACK

T he Shak kennels began to fill up quickly and things continued to progress well, as Stephen could now devote all his time to the charity. He didn't have to worry any longer about maintaining two jobs so the pressure on him eased, and rescued dogs began to trickle out the other end of the Shak process. He worked full-time and shared out-of-hours duties with Gregg, who was now being paid part-time in addition to his job and studies. They also provided weekend cover for the council's collection service, the total of which they knew was likely to sap their energy and enthusiasm if it all continued too long.

Pretty soon it became obvious that the kennels were always going to fill up much faster than they were vacated at the other end of the system, so they squeezed in even more hours trying to keep up. Covering the whole of Northumberland was almost impossible for two men though, and their private and social lives quickly disappeared in a haze of mental and physical exhaustion.

It was impossible to plan family days or outings because they were inevitably interrupted by callouts, at which times Stephen had to either take the family home or with him to the rescue. Either choice ruined the day. Part-time volunteers did help but also had their own lives to live.

Extreme pressure began to descend once again as Stephen tried desperately to balance his life, but at that point he was fighting a losing battle. The stark choices were either neglecting his family or letting down animals in desperate need. Gregg was also seriously fed up and began to take time off, loading yet more work and responsibility onto his friend's shoulders.

Stephen was beginning to struggle as the workload mounted and family time vanished altogether, and it became evident that Elaine thought her husband was actively choosing his work over her and their daughter, because he enjoyed it more than being with them. She came to the conclusion that he preferred the company of his rescued dogs to that of his family.

'But Elaine,' he tried desperately to explain after abandoning yet another social event. 'That isn't the choice - the choice is either going to rescue the dogs or letting them die.'

But the hole he'd dug himself into got deeper and deeper until he couldn't see any way out. Had he created a monster, he asked himself? Had his dream turned into a nightmare rollercoaster that he couldn't get off?

More bad news arrived when a private kennel offered to take over the council callout service at a lower rate, which Shak had to match to even attempt to retain the contract. The council decided to split the work between the two kennels - one covering rural areas and the other urban. None of those options were attractive to the newcomer though, which proceeded to press for a total takeover, until it emerged that they only wanted to provide service during the winter months when kennel business was slow. But they strung things out long enough to cause months of painful uncertainty before finally withdrawing. By that time Gregg and his new girlfriend had tired of the whole situation, decided their happiness and long-term future lay in another direction, and pulled out. Their decision was hastened by the council insisting that although the competing kennel had dropped out of the running, the newly-agreed rates would stand.

Stephen now only had inexperienced assistance with cleaning and feeding, though his mother and her friends still persisted with their productive fundraising efforts.

He was on duty 15 hours per day, 7 days every week and had absolutely no time to himself or to spend with his family. Even if he managed to get home by midnight on occasion, he was too exhausted to do anything but sleep. The pressure on everybody increased to a crescendo but Stephen continued his refusal to ignore the needs of animals he was called on to help, and life began to slip out of his control. He became so tired and run down that after rescuing dogs late at night, he often resorted to bringing them home instead of to the kennels in order to save an hour or two, and take them the following morning instead. Unfortunately the only place to house them was in a crate positioned at the end of a corridor adjoining the lounge, which wasn't very popular with his long-suffering wife.

'Do you have to bring them all home with you every night?' she asked from the end of her severely stretched tether.

'It adds another two hours to my day if I go up to the kennels every night, and I've already done fifteen today, and I can't afford to lose what's left of the council contract or Shak will collapse.'

'You'll collapse if you carry on as you are!'

'Elaine, I'm just trying to hold everything together until it gets better.'

'It's not getting better Stephen, it's getting worse by the day and I just cannot stand it any longer, and it's not fair on our daughter - you always being too busy to spend any time with her.'

'So what am I supposed to do - just put all the dogs back on the kill-list?'

'Come on Stephen, you know I'd never want that to happen but something has to change.'

'I know, and I want things to change as much as you - do you think I like working around the clock twenty four seven, because I can assure you that I don't.'

She looked at him without reply.

'I'd absolutely love to have more time to spend with you both...and maybe even watch some football with a beer or two now and again.'

She still didn't speak.

'The cup final's coming up,' he added in self pity.

'So why don't you take time out to have a beer and watch the bloody football?' she asked with intense persuasion.

'Maybe because last time I sat down to watch the cup final my bloody phone rang two minutes into the match and I had to go out on a call,' he smiled.

Elaine was about to return his smile when as if on cue, his phone rang. He answered it as she levelled a seething stare at him, before getting up and walking away.

Twenty Four

MISS BLUE STAR

Stephen thought hard about everything he could lose if he didn't prevent it, and looked for any little ways he might improve the situation. His mother was fundraising outside Jollyes pet store at West Denton one day and Elaine was helping, along with Neve. He planned his day meticulously so he could call in whilst passing, and spend half an hour with them all. While there he received a callout saying, 'There's a dog dying in a garden at Ashington.'

'Okay, give me the address,' he replied, dropping everything and rushing off because he suspected an organised dog-fight was in progress.

He parked the truck and walked quickly along a pedestrian-only terrace, to a boarded-up house surrounded by waist-high grass and weeds. Moving around the perimeter he couldn't see anything and was about to leave, when he heard a faint whimper so clambered over the fence and intensified his search. Curled up in a small, black, furry ball was a dog which he could see was a very young, female Lurcher when she stood as he approached. She was quite tall and leggy and bared her teeth in feeble defiance as Stephen held out a hand, but relaxed a little when she realised the hand held a hot-dog sausage. He managed to slip a lead over her head as she ravenously devoured the dog delicacy, and was able to coax the frozen, starving and saturated animal out of the garden.

He took her home and was drying her off with a warm towel when Elaine and Neve arrived back. Neve walked into the kitchen, saw the bedraggled but handsome dog and her eyes lit up.

'It looks just like our Miss Blue Sky but a different colour,' she said.

'She's a little girl as well,' Stephen added.

'What's she called?'

'She hasn't got a name yet; what do you think about calling her…umm…maybe Star because stars and the sky go together don't they.'

'Star, yes – Miss Blue Star, they'll be just like twin sisters!'

A week later Star fell ill from being so thin and malnourished, and Stephen took her to see Jonathan at Moorview Vets where she was immediately admitted for tests. She was confined for 8 days during which time she lost even more weight, before Jonathan telephoned to say that the kindest option would be to end her suffering now.

'Can I bring my daughter to say goodbye first - they became quite fond of each other during the short time Star was with us?'

'Yes, that's fine but can you bring her today?'

Stephen went home, broke the sad news to Neve and took her to say farewell to Star that afternoon. They decided it would be nicer for them to meet outside in the sunshine than in the clinical operating room where the dog was about to die, and Star was led out already looking half-dead and hardly able to stand.

But then something strange happened - Star saw Neve and an immediate spark of life from their previously burgeoning friendship passed between them. Neve smiled and walked forward with her arms out, and Star actually play-bowed before nuzzling into her embrace.

'That's amazing,' said Jonathan, letting go of the lead.

'They love each other,' added Stephen.

'Maybe she's not as close to death as we thought.'

'She probably gave up hope when we parted them.'

'Possibly.'

'So maybe she deserves another chance?'

'Mm, alright we'll give her another two days and see what happens, but if she continues to refuse food it leaves us no other choice.'

The vet took Star back inside and Stephen took his daughter home, and at 5.30 the same afternoon received a call.

'That'll be another callout,' he said, clicking his phone on.

'Hi Stephen, it's Jonathan here.'

'Bad news already?'

'On the contrary and you might not believe this, but for the first time in nine days your little dog has started eating!'

From that point forward Star made such rapid progress that 3 days later she was back in Bedlington with the Wylies, lying on the rug in front of the television with her saviour - little Neve. The young girl was hooked on being an animal rescuer as she loved to call her daddy, punching a tiny fist in the air, and going out on calls with him at weekends.

One Saturday afternoon he got a request to collect an old Labrador which was wandering to and fro across Cowpen Road in Blyth. A lady from a nearby care-home had seen it, so coaxed it into the garden and shut the gate. 'It's an old dog at an old folks' home,' she laughed.

Neve was dressed as a fairy complete with gossamer wings at the time, having a tea party in the garden at home with her teddy-bears. She heard the telephone conversation and asked, 'Can I come, daddy?'

'I haven't time to wait for you to get changed, Nevey.'

'That's alright daddy, I can be a fairy animal rescuer for today!'

Stephen smiled and asked Elaine, 'What do you think, there's an old dog down at Blyth - we'll be there and back in half an hour?'

'Okay but be careful you two brave animal rescuers.'

They tucked Neve and her wings into the cab and set off for Blyth in the truck, where a staff member directed the dynamic duo to the home's rear garden. The aged Lab was wandering aimlessly, looking very unkempt with years of dirt and matting clogging his yellow coat, and unsteady on all four legs. On closer inspection he had infected ears which oozed black wax, some rotten teeth and cataracts in both eyes.

'I don't think he can see very well,' Neve whispered so the dog wouldn't be offended, and gave him a big hug.

Stephen grimaced and said, 'Don't get those wings dirty, you've only got one pair so you'll be grounded if they don't work properly!'

The staff member smiled but said, 'He's not in very good shape is he.'

'No, he looks pretty bad.'

'So what will happen to him, will he have to be put to sleep?'

'No we don't do that, do we Neve?'

'No we don't, we're animal rescuers so he can come home with us, can't he daddy?'

'Really?' exclaimed the carer in surprise, looking at the dog's grimy condition.

'Yes, sick dogs come to our house all the time.'

'Well I'm not sure mum will be over the moon about this particular one,' Stephen frowned. 'But I suppose we can give it a shot for a while at least until we sort him out a bit.'

Neve and the carer were extremely pleased but Stephen was apprehensive on the drive home.

'Oh no, not another one,' Elaine protested as the animal rescue team helped the old dog out of the truck. 'And look at the state of it!'

'Well…yes but it was Neve's decision,' Stephen offered in cowardly mitigation with a crooked smile on his face.

During a routine medical check it was discovered that the unfortunate dog also had testicular cancer, and the Wylie rescue committee decided he'd have to stay a little longer to see if anything could be done for him.

'Well if he's staying he needs a damn good wash at least,' declared Elaine to her daughter, sitting in the garden watching the bedraggled dog.

'Yes he does, he's very dusty isn't he.'

'Yes he is – *very* dusty.'

'So should we call him Dusty?'

Twenty Five
DUDLEY

There were now four dogs with complications in the house in addition to the many and varied needs of a three year-old child, all of which placed increased pressure on Elaine. Surely there's no room for any more, she hoped, but then Stephen received a call from Lisa at New Hope Rescue in Gravesend, Kent. A very underweight German Shepherd had been found abandoned in the wilderness of St Mary's Marshes, out in the Thames estuary.

'He can't even stand properly,' Lisa reported. 'There's no muscle at all around his back end so it looks like he might have CDRM. He'd definitely have died out there if he hadn't been spotted.'

'He'll need special attention by the sound of things.'

'I know, that's why I called you.'

'Well I've had some experience of it but I can't work miracles, you have to understand?'

'But can you take him?'

There wasn't a moment's hesitation before Stephen replied, 'Yes I can and fortunately, one of our volunteers is down your way on personal business next week so I'm sure she'll pick him up.'

Dudley arrived in Northumberland the following Sunday in horrendous condition. He was filthy, crippled and Stephen felt immediate empathy and a connection to him. Elaine was horrified at the sight of the hapless, abused dog but agreed he could stay for one night.

On first inspection Stephen was almost certain that the dog had the terrible wasting disease that plagued the hind legs and haunches of the breed, and now that he was in full control of a case, was interested in exploring different therapies including podiatric footwear, supportive harnesses, dog wheelchairs, massage and particularly - hydrotherapy. He'd recently been researching its many techniques and their benefits with Trevor at 4Paws, such as leading a dog in swimming to the right if addressing problems on its right side, and vice-versa for the left.

Dudley became a project in progress and a very close bond developed between him and Stephen, and the one-night stay stipulated by Elaine stretched into weeks.

Stephen involved Neve as much as possible and she loved watching the weekly swim sessions, saying poor Dudley looked so loveable with his head bobbing in the water and paws thrashing in front of him. He hated the pool at first but soon grew to love it and showed rapid improvement in his general health and condition. From paws dragging and screeching on the tiles as they coaxed him into the pool first time, he progressed to clambering straight over the barrier to get in the water as soon as possible. Stephen had to hold a canine lifejacket open at the back of the truck as Dudley was let out, so he ran straight into it on his eager way to his favourite pastime.

As Stephen watched him swimming around faster and faster he knew the rescued dog was happy, and that made him smile. Dudley's needs were those of a disabled child as he had to be helped with almost everything. He also needed lots of short duration exercise which all added time to Stephen's day, as well as great satisfaction, and eventually it became clear that a serious rift was opening up between him and his wife. He tried to create more time to spend with her but his dogs' needs repeatedly got in the way, and Elaine retreated to the safe territory of her job, her daughter and the stable, predictable parts of her life.

Stephen continued along the unswerving path he'd wholly committed to, and to the learning journey its successful navigation required. He took Dudley to the beach at Cambois regularly to walk him on the soft sand, threw balls for him to chase at his own speed and watched him run free, and though the crippled dog's zest for life brought a tear to his eye, he was proud of Dudley and proud of himself and his charity for helping it to happen.

Sometimes the dog had toilet accidents in the house when he couldn't get up fast enough to make the door in time, and one day Elaine came in before Stephen had time to clean up. She was tired, immediately angry and said, 'I'm sick of coming home after a long day at work to this mess.'

'It's not his fault, Elaine.'

'I don't care whose fault it is - I just cannot carry on like this any longer.'

'So what do you expect me to do?'

'Put him in the kennels where he belongs - he was only supposed to be here one night and it's been weeks.'

'That can't happen Elaine, he'd never survive in the kennels in his condition and anyway, Neve and me love him now.'

'Yes, I'm quite sure you love all your dogs, and the only thing you don't love around here is your wife.'

Stephen was trapped between two very strong emotional ties and although he knew the possible if not probable consequences, he could not bring himself to betray the trust of Dudley or any of the other dogs he'd committed so much of his life to saving. He fully understood Elaine's unhappiness as the relatively successful man she'd married and had a child with, abruptly changed so completely and radically but without a doubt, giving life to condemned dogs was now the mission in his life and he went about it with the same zeal and efficiency he'd applied to selling telephones.

He tried to explain his dilemma to Elaine, including the fact that he did still love her, but she wasn't prepared to accept the massive and progressive changes to her life. She became more and more unhappy and distanced herself from him and unavoidably, their differences deteriorated into arguments. The bickering continued and intensified until one day Elaine said calmly, 'Look Stephen, if you love your dogs so much, why don't you move out and go live with them at the kennels?'

That was the start of a steep, downhill slide in the marriage, but neither could afford to set up a new home and Stephen didn't want to walk out on his daughter's childhood. Elaine understood that and didn't want Neve to miss out on her father's presence, so agreed that they could continue living separate lives in the same house. The dogs which needed to, stayed and Stephen continued his very positive relationship with Neve. Elaine started to enjoy other things in life and it became clear that their marriage was well and truly over.

In early December that year Stephen was driving home from the kennels with Dudley in the back of the truck. The dog had been unwell earlier in the day and recovered, but Stephen didn't want to leave him alone. Before they got home he received two callouts, one straight after the other. The first was from the council regarding a Golden Retriever which had been found by a resident and taken to a flat in Cramlington, a few miles west of Blyth. He attended the flat where a young woman told him she'd found the dog wandering alone in Alexandria Park, to the rear of Southfield Green and perhaps significantly - bordering Dudley Lane.

That's a coincidence, he thought, remembering that Dudley was still in the back of the truck as he checked the Retriever for a micro-chip. He didn't find one so gave the woman her two options:

'Well look er...'

'Rachel.'

'Look Rachel, you can keep him overnight or I have to take him to the kennels now?'

'Oh no,' she replied. 'It's freezing outside and I've just got him warmed up and settled. I'll feed him and keep him here until you can locate his owner.'

'Okay but you must understand that the owner has seven days to claim the dog, and it must be returned to him if he does.'

'That's fine; I hope he's claimed soon,' Rachel agreed, feeding treats to the Retriever and her own Border Collie cross - Nima.

'If it isn't claimed within seven days he'll be picked up by the local warden but you could always apply for adoption.'

She decided to keep the dog for the time being and asked Stephen about the Shak tee-shirt he was wearing. He explained all about his charity and they chatted for a while before he left on the next callout, which was to collect an apparently lost West Highland Terrier. The little Westy was chipped so he took it straight home after a phone call to check it was still wanted there. He then got yet another call to say that the Retriever's owner had just come forward, so it could also be returned.

He went back to Rachel's flat, explained that the owner had been in touch, and they continued their conversation about Shak. She was nearing the end of a degree course in Alternative Therapies, and was very interested because she intended to carry it forward to incorporate a second qualification, in Alternative Therapies for Animals. He told her about Dudley and his needs before leaving with the Retriever, promising to keep in touch.

A few days later he telephoned to ask if she was serious about visiting Shak, and also whether she might help with Dudley's treatment. She was genuinely keen and the following week Stephen took the dog to Rachel's flat for a trial massage. He loved it, the muscle relaxation definitely helped his mobility, and he also got along quite well with Nima. A week later Stephen took her to meet Trevor at 4Paws to learn more about hydrotherapy, and their new friendship seemed to be working out well for both of them.

Twenty Six

NEVE

Living as virtual strangers in the same house with Elaine didn't work out and was in danger of affecting Neve. Her parents spoke to each other but only when necessary and certainly not with any affection. Stephen felt an increasing need to break away from the situation and found himself absently browsing the local property pages, even though he knew he'd struggle to afford a place on his own anything like the Bedlington cottage he loved.

'Moving house?' asked friend and Shak supporter Yvonne, as he flipped the pages of the Northumberland Gazette.

'If only,' he answered with a sigh.

'Is there a problem? You look a bit down in the dumps.'

'Oh, it's a long story Yvonne. I just need a break from everything and everybody, somewhere on my own for a little while.'

'Well there's been a cancellation on one of the log cabins up at Fram Park; you could hide away up there for a fortnight?'

'That sounds like an idea, I'll have to have a think about that.'

'Well don't take too long, they're very popular.'

He decided to accept the offer and took Dudley with him. The dog's health had deteriorated, it now couldn't walk far and was consequently depressed, and the two spent a few evenings quietly comforting each other after Stephen finished work each day. In the early mornings they went for short walks and discovered that Dudley liked splashing around in the River Coquet near Rothbury, but one frosty morning as they set out together, the dog collapsed. Stephen carried him back to the cabin, placed him in the back of the truck and took him straight to the vet, who found a tumour pressing on his spinal chord. Nothing could be done to cure him, and the kindest option was to put him to sleep there and then to save him suffering any more pain. Stephen went back to the cabin alone feeling deep sadness for the loss of his friend, to also contemplate the facts that his marriage had failed, he was virtually homeless and in danger of losing contact with his daughter.

He met up with Rachel one day that had been arranged for Dudley's weekly massage therapy; she could see how upset he was and offered to help. They talked for hours but this time also included themselves, their lives and what each of them hoped for in the future.

Returning to the Bedlington house was difficult for Stephen after tasting freedom from the stress and anguish for a fortnight, and he decided he had to make a permanent move sooner rather than later. He stepped up his property search but failed to find anywhere he could afford, that was suitable and would accept 4 dogs. One estate agent made the worrying assumption that he'd willingly cut down to 2 dogs or even 1, to find a new home but of course that would never be the case.

'Oh I see,' she said when Stephen explained his lifetime mission. 'I think I might've read about you in the Gazette.'

'Possibly,' he replied.

'Well actually, we might have somewhere suitable - it's a farmhouse way out in the countryside.'

'That sounds promising, can I have a look?'

A viewing was arranged and whilst being shown around the property by the farmer who owned it, Stephen commented, 'It's a fantastic place but probably far too big for just me on my own.'

'Mm, I was thinking that myself but as it happens, I do have another place that might suit you better.'

'Yeah?'

'Yes, it's not as big and has some land attached, but it's a bit of a hike getting to it.'

'Where is it?'

'It's right at the top of Castle Hill near Alnham, you know the ancient settlement site?'

'I've heard of it but never been there.'

'And of course the rent's a good bit less than the big place, but there is a slight problem.'

'Yeah?'

'Yeah, I've been refurbishing it and the place is like a bomb-site at the moment.'

'Can I have a look anyway?'

Stephen loved the cottage as soon as he saw it and the surrounding views, and heard the silent tranquillity of its remote setting. He agreed to take it there and then, picturing the freedom his growing household of dogs would enjoy, and hardly even noticed the building work debris. He was excited about moving to a new home and completely new lifestyle where for instance, his water was supplied by a stream and heat provided by fallen branches collected in the nearby woods. At the same time he was sad to leave Neve and the place he'd called home for over 10 years, and in the final analysis - disappointed that his marriage to a woman he'd truly loved had come to an end. But he knew he was moving to more than a new home and lifestyle - he was embarking on a real adventure which could also include Neve and provide her with experiences she would never otherwise have.

Life on Castle Hill was from a bygone era, when everything had to be planned in advance because there were no shops for miles around and convenience-living didn't exist. Even getting to and from home was problematic in winter because driven snow would often block off the whole lower part of the house, including the doors and windows. At such times Stephen had to leave the truck at the bottom of the long, winding lane and walk the last mile or so through snow-drifts sometimes over a metre deep. In an emergency he'd detour the truck through a couple of gates and plough through the fields once he was acquainted with the sub-snow terrain. In winter the focus was on survival and resembled life in Scandinavia.

During less extreme weather Neve visited at weekends and loved the rural location. Her father's friendship with Rachel had blossomed into a relationship and she brought her own daughter, Grace to spend time at the cottage. The girls loved going off exploring the woods, and carrying back bundles of sticks for cosy evenings around the cast-iron stove. On one occasion Stephen recognised a neighbouring farmer's fence posts heading for the flames, and rescued them just in time.

The girls played outside in the fresh air for hours and never looked at a screen of any kind. In fact, Stephen didn't even install a television because he didn't want the distraction when he first moved, and became so used to not having one that he never bothered afterwards. When the little group gathered on the hilltop they were more than happy basking in the seclusion, appreciating the stunning views and the joys of light-hearted conversation, and watching the dogs enjoying freedom.

In the late evening Rachel would sometimes wander off across the fields and sit on an old dry-stone wall, to watch the crystal clear moon light up the landscape as Stephen followed with a bottle of wine. On summer evenings they might pitch a tent behind the house and they'd all sit out, laughing and chatting until the girls fell asleep and dreamed about this less complicated lifestyle.

'Life must've been really nice in the olden days,' Neve said to Stephen one morning as they set off on the drive back to civilization.

'Some of it,' he agreed. 'But there were lots of hard times as well.'

'How come?'

'Well for example, only about fifty years ago the man who lived in this very house was a shepherd, and he'd been out with two other men when it started snowing really hard, and the shepherd got home but his two friends were lost in the storm.'

'That must've been frightening.'

'Yes, so you just be careful when you're out there collecting firewood with Grace.'

'What was his name, the man who lived here?'

'It was er, William Bulloch if I remember rightly, and he'd been to the Saturday farmers' market at Rothbury, with his friends on their tractor.'

'All that way on a tractor?'

'They probably didn't have cars and it was much too far to walk.'

'So what happened?'

'Well, on their way back they dropped Mr Bulloch off here and then carried on towards their own homes at Ewartly Shank, up in a remote part of the Cheviot Hills.'

'We can see them from your house can't we.'

'We can,' he answered, glancing at the towering ridges in the rear-view mirror. 'I can still see Cushat Law from here.'

'Oh yes,' she agreed, turning around to look.

'A blizzard blew up and that winter - 1962 to 63, was one of the coldest since records began and the road was just a narrow track back then so was soon covered over.'

'What were the other men called, dad?'

'One was Jock Scott and the other was Willie Middlemas, and in those days nobody up here had telephones.'

'What about mobiles?'

'They hadn't even been invented then and neither had PCs. Good job I wasn't born in those days or I wouldn't have had my shop!'

'Maybe you'd have been a shepherd?'

'Maybe,' he laughed.

'So how did people keep in touch with each other?'

'Just by letter mostly, but I'm not sure the postman could make it up here during winter.'

'So what happened when the other men got home?'

'Well, on Monday the shepherd was out in the fields tending his sheep, when Mr Scott's wife came along and asked if her husband was still with him.

"No," he replied, "Jock and Willie went straight home after dropping me off."

"Well I've not seen either of them since Saturday morning," Mrs Scott said, and then they both knew something bad must've happened so they raised the alarm.'

'What had happened?'

'They didn't know but the police, the RAF, local shepherds and farmers all formed search parties and found the tractor stuck in deep snow by the track. Mr

Scott's body was found under a big snowdrift on Tuesday, only half a mile from his home, and on Wednesday Mr Middlemas was found a hundred yards away from his friend.'

'Oh no.'

'I'm afraid so.'

'It's a really sad story isn't it.'

'It is but at least some good came of it.'

'Did it?'

'Yes, their deaths led to the Northumberland mountain rescue service being set up, and there's now a memorial cairn on High Knowes, close to where they died.'

'That's nice.'

'Yeah, the rescue team's called out at least once a week during summer, and more often in winter. At the time the newspapers ran stories about the tragedy and funds were raised for the bereaved families.'

'That's nice as well.'

'Mm, most people don't realise how dangerous it can be up here. The weather can be really wild in winter and the hills are exposed. A hundred years ago, a young girl called Nellie Herron set off from where she worked at Alnham, over the moors to her home at Hartside in the Ingram Valley, and was found sitting on a stone where she'd stopped to rest - frozen to death!'

'The poor thing.'

'Yes, and I'm not telling you these things to frighten you, I'm telling you so you'll always be careful and never wander off too far on your own, even if one of the dogs runs away.'

'I won't, I promise; well not *too* far anyway.'

DEDICATED
IN MEMORY OF
THE SHEPHERDS
JOCK SCOTT · WILLIE MIDDLEMAS
WHO PERISHED HERE IN THE SNOW
17th NOVEMBER 1962

ERECTED BY
NORTHUMBERLAND NATIONAL PARK AUTHORITY
AND NNP MOUNTAIN RESCUE TEAM

Twenty Seven

BODIE

S hak was based closer to Alnwick than any other
major town and as Stephen took in more dogs, he
and the charity became better known there. He also
met lots of people from the wider area; Shak became
quite a talking point and when the rural community
realised what he was trying to do, significantly more
donations came in. Even the local post-woman poked £20
through his letter-box with the mail each month. The
regional media soon showed an interest and Shak was
featured in the Northumberland Gazette, which also set
up a competition called the Jam Jar Army. Readers

nominated their favourite charities, and the one with most votes was awarded all the spare coinage which had been tossed into jam jars by the voters over previous months. Shak beat all previous winners by a wide margin which brought extra publicity, and eventually a weekly column in the paper.

Reports on the horrific treatment suffered by most of the dogs that Stephen rescued, shocked many and boosted interest in the unique charity even more, and further afield. Stephen was regularly recognised on the streets or out and about doing his work, and general awareness of the problems which exist around unwanted dogs increased rapidly.

Various volunteers had given up their time and worked hard to build up Shak's accommodation, welfare facilities and operations over preceding years, but with the charity growing so fast it became increasingly obvious that full-time assistance was needed. The volunteers had also increased collections of food and bedding donations, trips to the vet, cleaning of kennels and compounds and fundraising under the staunch leadership of Stephen's mother.

Shak could never have evolved as it did and into what it became without their ongoing help, but Stephen now needed constant staff who were in post at least 5 days every week, and could therefore be trained to perform more intricate and dangerous tasks in direct contact with the dogs. He would never put a volunteer at risk although many of them were well up for the challenge.

Joan and loyal assistant

One of the very first helpers was a teenager who came for 8 weeks via the Benefits system, as part of a work placement programme. Melissa received no payment or extra Benefits and worked more hours than she had to, and after her placement asked to be kept on as a volunteer. She was a good worker and could handle all the dogs, and was also reliable and willing to tackle anything asked of her, including scrubbing kennel floors soiled by nervous animals.

Melissa was an obvious candidate for full-time employment and when offered the opportunity, she accepted immediately. Stephen wasn't at first certain he could scrape together sufficient funds to pay her the minimum wage each week, but accepted that as yet another considerable challenge because his dogs needed her. It proved to be a good decision and Melissa's presence allowed him more time away from kennel duties to help raise much-needed funding.

Another work placement seeker arrived in the form of David, also in his teens and still living with his parents. Worryingly, considering where he'd been sent to work, David was terrified of German Shepherds and most other large breeds, as he'd been frightened by one as a child. In spite of that he loved animals and had always wanted a dog of his own, but his parents wouldn't allow it for their own reasons which possibly contributed to his fears.

'I don't think you'll like it here or be suitable for us,' Stephen told him on his first day at the kennels.

'I…I'd like to try, if that's alright?' he replied.

'Why's that?' Stephen asked, suspecting mere compliance with the Benefits system as the reason.

'Well…because I love dogs but never been allowed to have one, and I think it's something I could be good at.'

'We don't have any cuddly little puppies here you know?'

'I know.'

'We just have big scary dogs that nobody else wants.'

'I know.'

'But you still want to give it a go?'

'Yes please, Mr Wylie.'

Stephen looked at the youth for a long moment, recalling the years he himself was not allowed a dog, and reassessing his initial impressions before saying, 'Okay, come with me.'

David followed his potential boss into the howling, barking pandemonium which erupted when a stranger entered the kennels. Stephen handed him a lead, opened a gate and pointed to a big German Shepherd.

'This is Bodie,' Stephen said. 'His brother over there is Doyle.'

'O…okay,' David replied nervously.

'They were both scrapyard guard dogs and one day away from a bullet in the head when we got to them, so get in there,' Stephen instructed, knowing the dog was now completely harmless but not disclosing that information. 'Put the lead on and take him out for a walk.'

'I…er…are you sure?'

'Sure I'm sure, get yourself in there.'

David crept into the kennel slowly and carefully, clicked the lead onto Bodie's collar and took him out for a half-hour walk with no trouble. He walked him regularly after that and developed a love for big dogs.

Doyle

David had previously worked in catering and when his 8 weeks' placement was over, he took up employment as commis-chef at a hotel in Warkworth, near the castle on the A1068 northwest of Amble. He immediately missed working at Shak but kept in touch, bought himself a 125cc motor bike and travelled back and forth to continue volunteering on his days off.

'David turned out alright,' Stephen commented to Rachel as they swept out the kennels together one Sunday morning. 'It's a pity we can't take him on full-time as well as Melissa because they work well together.'

'Maybe you could.'

'We can't afford it I'm afraid, Rachel.'

'Have you ever considered applying for funding?'

'How do you mean - applying to who?'

'There are various charitable foundations around; many contribute to caring for children or the elderly and causes like that.'

'I've never heard of any supporting elderly dogs though?'

'You'll never know until you try.'

'True, so you think it's worth a shot?'

'Yes, you definitely need more help so what have you got to lose?'

'Nothing I suppose.'

'The only problem might be that normally they're not keen on funding long-term projects, they prefer to give specific amounts for one-off requirements such as buying new equipment or accommodation, or anything with an immediate visible benefit.'

'So that could be a problem?'

'Mm, could be. Remember the local guy we were talking to at the charities conference last year?'

'Erm…'

'The one who was asking you all about Shak.'

'Oh yeah, he was genuinely interested - a real dog-lover.'

'Well he was from a foundation if I remember correctly, so it might be worth applying to that one.'

'Which one was it?'

'Can't remember now, can you?'

'Nah, it was a year ago.'

'We could check the attendance list online and see if any of the names ring a bell?'

'Okay, as you say, it's worth a shot so let's do it.'

They trawled through the list that night and finally agreed on the Stewart Halbert Foundation, based at Haltwhistle in southwest Northumberland, close to the Vindolanda Museum on the Roman Wall. They skimmed through the documentation, discovering that the Foundation was set up in memory of Mr Stewart Halbert, an industrial oils magnate and creator of the global company, Kilfrost. It included Animal Welfare on its list of possible benefactors, so they prepared a detailed application, itemising Shak's value to society, submitted it and waited nervously for a reply, knowing they were not entitled to any explanation for refusal.

Twenty Eight

A DOG'S LIFE

During the tense, stressful period before leaving his Bedlington home, Stephen often retreated to his bedroom, opened his tablet and got through a few lonely hours writing. He began by recording many of the horrors suffered by the dogs he rescued, as justification for what had happened to him and his family as a consequence of helping them. It reinforced his determination to carry on and reminded him exactly why he had to. Eventually he strung the recorded events together chronologically, to form a story from the viewpoints of some of the dogs he'd known and loved over recent years. It was simply an exercise for his own satisfaction and he had no plans for the story beyond that, but it did serve to sharpen his mind to the problems and pitfalls of various situations.

After moving to Castle Hill a woman telephoned him one day about a 5 year-old dog she'd adopted from a rescue shelter, asking if she could visit to discuss a problem.

'So how can I help you?' Stephen asked when they met.

'Well, I need to get rid of the dog because it keeps peeing in the house and ruining my carpets, and the shelter certainly never mentioned anything about that before I paid them.'

'How long have you had the dog?'

'Only a week or two but it's already become an intolerable nuisance. This is definitely not what I had in mind but the shelter says if I take the dog back there they'll probably end up putting it to sleep, and I wouldn't want that for the poor thing.'

'What's it like apart from peeing in the house?'

'Well, it's alright I suppose. It's actually a lovely dog which is why I chose it in the first place, but I can't put up with that sort of behaviour, not at my age.'

'But if it's only been there a week it'll still be settling in.'

'Settling in? It's a dog for Heaven's sake and I've given it a wonderful home. It was a stray, out on the streets before that.'

'But it doesn't know that yet and it'll still be very nervous.'

'Excuse me?'

'It doesn't know that you've given it a home and has no idea what to expect, except something bad again so you have to give it more time.'

'So where exactly does it think it is then, in your opinion?'

'It has no idea. It might be a beautiful home but that won't register with the dog. Dog's are only interested in who they're with, not the colour of the curtains.'

'B...but it must realise it's now somewhere vastly better than those horrid kennels it was in?'

'Yes but it doesn't realise yet that it's not going back there.'

The lady paused for a second and Stephen continued, 'Try to imagine the situation from the dog's perspective - it was probably enjoying life in its previous home, but something happened and it was dumped on the street where it was cold, lonely, probably starving and very frightened. Then it was manhandled by a dog-warden and locked in a cage at the local pound, where it was isolated completely on its own for a week before being transferred to the general kennels and surrounded by dozens of other terrified dogs, barking and howling for hours on end. From there it would be moved to the re-homing block and taken out for short walks by a succession of different people, but caged up again each time afterwards.'

Stephen paused for breath and the lady continued to stare at him with large, round, watery eyes.

'And then,' he continued softly. 'You came along and took him to your house expecting him to be grateful, which he will be if you give him the chance. But at the moment he doesn't know where he is or for how long or even why he's there. He's at the end hopefully, of a major disruption to his life but he's completely confused and extremely nervous, because although you've adopted him he doesn't realise that. You're still a stranger to him and he has absolutely no idea that you want to offer him a good home and look after him for the rest of his life.'

They stood silently looking at each other for a very long moment, before the lady spoke:

'Well…' she began as Stephen prepared himself for an angry response.

'I must say that you've explained that extremely well and you're obviously right. I'd never imagined for one second what it must all be like from the dog's point of view.'

Stephen smiled but said nothing.

'I've decided to give him another chance if you'll promise me that I can telephone you for advice if I need to?'

'Of course you can, anytime and if you like I can always come to visit.'

'Thank you so much Mr Wylie, you've put my troubled mind at rest.'

She did keep in touch and let Stephen know that her dog made rapid progress and had such a wonderful nature, that within a few months he was registered with Pets as Therapy (PAT), visiting care homes around the area and cheering up the residents. She asked Stephen to come along one evening and give one of his inspirational talks, which led on to him taking selected dogs of his own to evenings at care homes, scouts and guides meetings, schools, women's institutes and various other venues where he gave talks and presentations. The recipients were almost always mesmerised by the facts and the calmness of the once-troubled dogs, and appreciated Stephen's knowledge, expertise and down-to-earth delivery. Extra donations flooded in along with invitations and commendations, and of course increasing demands on his time. He slotted in as many events as possible, and respect for him and the charity he'd created grew immensely.

'People like what they hear from you,' Rachel told him one evening as they sipped wine in the back garden after a long day at the kennels.

'I just tell it like it is,' he replied.

'Well you should tell as many people as possible.'

'I'm doing as much as I can manage and a bit more besides.'

'What about going online again, starting a blog or something?'

They decided to write a short piece to put out on social media, pleading with people not to get rid of their dogs too soon because of problems which could easily be solved, and offered various snippets of advice. It was supposed to be just a couple of paragraphs but the brimming wealth of knowledge in Stephen's head could not be squeezed into those parameters. He kept on typing and realised that he was actually repeating much of the story he'd started back in Bedlington, and retrieved the printed script from the bottom of a still-unpacked bag. He resumed the semi-fictional tale and Rachel persuaded him to let her read it. The story contained some brutal parts but overall she loved it, recognising real dogs and situations on the pages, and encouraged him to carry on. He did so, proof-read it several times and managed to get it produced by a north-east publisher, which attracted yet more positive publicity.

Elaine knew he'd started writing before he left, but not that he'd finished the project. She, her mother and Neve, who did know, were walking past Waterstone's bookshop in Blackett Street, Newcastle one day whilst out shopping, and Neve slowed to scan the window.

'Mum,' she shouted and both adults stopped.

'Look, there's dad's book – *It's a Dog's Life!*'

Stephen gave his daughter a copy and on World Book Day at school a few weeks later, she carried it proudly, dressed as a rescued dog. Her teachers were surprised as they didn't know about the book, and Stephen was pleased when she told him all about it in fine detail.

More good news arrived when the Stewart Halbert Foundation accepted Shak's application, and awarded funding in the form of one year's minimum wage payment. David the trainee chef was offered a full-time, paid post and he accepted immediately. He and Melissa resumed working together and also formed a romantic relationship. He left the constraints of his parents' home behind and they moved into a flat together, and began saving to get married. The charity continued to grow but as more and more rescued dogs used the equipment and facilities, Stephen noticed that much of it was now starting to deteriorate quite rapidly. One problem solved but many others on the way, he realised.

Twenty Nine

A TAN STAFFIE

S hak continued to thrive and built up to an average 60 dogs at any one time. Donations were given and fundraising kept a trickle of money coming in, but not fast enough to keep pace with the growth of the charity. Stephen's vision had begun to resonate with caring people who wanted to help, but as it grew so did associated costs and expenses. To make matters much worse, the original facilities and hardware that Stephen inherited when he took over the site, continued to decay and were failing fast.

The wire barrier fencing that previously housed retired Greyhounds, which when not racing are relaxed, laid-back animals, was simply not strong enough to withstand the stresses and strains imposed on it by the new residents, who would constantly dispel their restrained energy by bouncing and crashing up against it whenever a stranger happened by.

The kennel gates were constructed from 50mm diameter, mild steel tubular bars, which were spaced just far enough apart for inquisitive canines to poke a paw or muzzle through at unsuspecting visitors, who were often taken unawares and more than a little surprised. The gates needed to be replaced to comply with health & safety legislation even just for the staff. In addition, the steel was not galvanised or rust-proofed and as a result was in constant decay leading to repeated fractures.

The barriers between cages were also in a state of collapse following increased use and stress, and failure could expose a frightened, abused dog to one which was also fearful, but coped with it by displaying defensive aggression towards anything within its immediate safety zone. General maintenance became impossible without component renewal, which would be very expensive.

'Everything alright?' Stephen asked Rachel with some concern as he re-entered the kennels, after a strained meeting with the vet to discuss a further extension of credit on Shak's ever-mounting account.

'Not really,' she answered, wrestling with a large kennel gate which had broken free from its fetters. 'All the staff are out walking dogs so I thought I'd tackle this on my own, but it's very awkward.'

He grabbed one side of the gate and helped re-position it in the opening, lifted it onto two wooden blocks to raise the bottom rail above the muddy ground, and then turned towards the little cabin used as an office.

'Just hang onto it so it doesn't fall over again,' he said, and quickly returned with a handful of plastic cable-ties.

Fastening one to the top and bottom of the hinge-post, he looped them around the gate's vertical rail, rendering it at least operable and reasonably safe, and they tied it shut with a length of string.

'I'll put a slip-knot in it,' Stephen said with a smile. 'So it's easier to get in and out.'

'We can't go on like this though,' she replied sadly. 'It's all going to fall down around us if we don't do something.'

'I know but we're just so short of money at the moment. The grant ran out this month so we've two wages to find now on top of everything else.'

'Why don't we apply for more funding?'

'I was thinking about that but just never had the time lately.'

'I have some more bad news.'

'Oh no, what now?'

'The washer's making a strange noise and the dryer's packed in altogether so we can't get any of the bedding clean, and it's November already so things can only get worse with winter coming on.'

'Right, let's make time and apply for some more funding this weekend.'

They worked late into Saturday and Sunday night to send off several applications, and eventually received a small award from Support Adoption for Pets – the charitable wing of Pets at Home, and also from the Kennel Club Charitable Trust.

'I didn't think we were going to get anything,' Rachel said with a beaming smile. 'After they both asked how many dogs we re-home each year.'

'Yeah, that was a tricky question but at least it gave us chance to emphasize that we are a unique charity in that we don't rescue just to re-home - we rescue to give life to dogs which would otherwise be put to sleep.'

'Maybe word really is getting out there to the big wide world at last?'

'We can only hope so and keep working at it.'

As soon as the money hit the bank account they replaced the central exercise runs which were falling apart, then searched online and found some second-hand, free-standing pens which could hold one or maybe two dogs each. They bought them and Joan's husband Mike put them together as they were transported flat-packed to further save costs. Mike had the necessary knowledge and tools, plenty of help from the volunteers and didn't deplete the treasured store of industrial strength cable-ties!

The pens were intended to be temporary until the available space could be utilised and managed more effectively, but soon became permanent fixtures as more and more dogs were rescued from certain death, after miserable lives. Lack of space soon crept up like a recurrent plague and overtook them again.

Stephen and the staff were now continually juggling and balancing everything in an ongoing struggle for survival, which caused a lot of stress and headaches for all concerned. At least one significant problem occurred every day and it became obvious that they were swimming against a very fast, incoming tide and losing the race.

On the recent upswing of Shak's popularity Stephen was interviewed several times on local television and in the press, and one day was invited as a guest speaker on Lionheart Radio, a volunteer-run service based in Alnwick town centre. He declined but later thinking it might be a way to publicise Shak as with the Jam Jar

Army, he agreed. He obviously had a talent for broadcasting, his choice of music was popular with listeners and he was asked back. He accepted again and was subsequently offered a permanent slot in the weekly timetable, which he named *It's a Dog's Life* after his book, and added an introductory jingle.

Stephen used every spare minute to search the news for dog-related stories, and transcribe them to report in between his favourite tunes. His slot's popularity grew rapidly and was rated the best show on station, and helped spread the word about Shak and the plight of condemned dogs. Unfortunately because of the recent cascade of increasing pressures at the kennels, he couldn't find time to continue with the new venture and had to sacrifice it, along with the many other things in his life over the years. His last dedication was a tear-jerking tribute to all the beloved dogs that had died, at least peacefully and after enjoying some happiness, at Shak.

The irritability and unrest amongst the staff became clear late one particular day, when another kennel gate with rusted hinges fell to the sodden ground. The Rottweiler inside had to be moved to the only other available pen and as the gate on that one was tied shut with damp string, Stephen's mobile rang. It was Eleanor from the vet's and he groaned, 'It's not about my account again is it?'

'No Stephen it's not, we've agreed to give you as much time as you need with that, haven't we?'

'That's what I thought?'

'Right, well no it's something completely different.'

'Go on?'

'We have a tan Staffie here whose owner wants him put down.'

'For what reason?'

'We can't get the real reason out of him but we can't see a problem with the dog. It seems fine if a little boisterous, but I know the guy's wife just had a baby.'

'Oh right, that one again - new baby in so poor little faithful dog out and up for the needle.'

'Looks like it, so can you take him?'

'I'll need a little time to sort some space, we're absolutely rammed.'

'Well it's getting late now so we'll keep him overnight, but if we don't have somewhere to place him by nine thirty tomorrow, I'll have no choice but to…you know what.'

'Okay, I'll be over there for nine in the morning.'

The staff heard some of the conversation and were looking at Stephen with blank expressions, knowing there was no room for even one more dog.

'Okay,' he said again, clapping his hands together. 'Let's get this place sorted out and some room made for a Staffie who's coming over tomorrow morning.'

There was a communal gasp of exasperation and one of the volunteers, Janet asked, 'But where can we put him? We've had to double two of the Lurchers up to make room for the Rotty and there's just nowhere else.'

Stephen paused for a moment, feeling a bit like Captain Bligh in front of the mutineers on the swaying deck of HMS Bounty, before clapping his hands again, louder this time and saying, 'Well let's get this broken pen repaired then.'

It was late in the day and the winter sky was darkening, and the staff members looked at each other in pained disbelief, but Rachel was already returning from the cabin with trusty cable-ties in hand. They followed her pro-active example and within half an hour the pen was operational again, and general demeanour within the

183

group had completely changed. They were pleased with their united success and left with triumphant smiles on their faces. Stephen was relieved and said to Rachel, 'Thank Christ you thought of that and it actually worked again.'

'No bother and why wouldn't it work?' she asked with a smile. 'We're cable-tie experts now aren't we?'

The tan Staffie was saved and quite quickly re-homed, but the same and similar problems re-occurred over the remaining weeks leading towards Christmas. As the weather worsened, water ran down the east hill slope and into the kennels enclosure, flooding the bare ground and turning it into a quagmire. The freestanding pens tilted every way possible and began to fall apart, and were patched together in a fashion using redundant mesh from the original partitions. Stephen was squelching around in the mud one afternoon, trying to feed and walk the dogs, when his mother popped her head around the edge of the corrugated-iron doorway.

'What on earth is going on?' she asked with a gasp of shocked dismay.

'Oh, we had a bit of a flood, mam,' he replied. 'And some of the cages are falling to bits.'

'Well you'll have to get some new ones, son.'

'That's the answer right enough but I'm afraid we can't afford to just yet.'

'But, money's still coming in isn't it?'

'It is but it's going out even faster now we've got more dogs to look after, and David's wage funding has stopped.'

'Oh dear, you never told me that.'

'I know, I didn't want to worry you.'

'Well you should have worried me before everything got into such a mess.'

'You're already doing as much as you can, mam, it's just getting harder and harder to keep up with it all.'

'Is this why you packed in your radio show?'

'Yeah, just didn't have time anymore. Can't expect the staff to be slaving away down here while I'm wittering away on the radio.'

'It was good publicity though but never mind, I'll have to do a bit more won't I, and raise some more funds to get us out of this mess.'

Joan did her best to increase income to Shak, had some early success and others raised more by various means, including Jill who set up a sales page on Facebook and worked hard to bring in regular funds from it. But as always approaching Christmas, cash donations dipped in favour of food, bedding, treats, toys and clothing; most of which was stored for later use. As New Year passed and January frost began to bite, all efforts were concentrated on keeping the dogs as comfortable as possible in the dark, damp atmosphere with no heating and little lighting.

Stephen stood in the dank gloom late one night, after his still-loyal staff left for the day, and knew that the end was close. It had to be because the life he was providing for his dogs was not good enough, and could only get a lot worse without some kind of miracle. He had no idea what that could be and didn't believe in miracles anyway, and knew he'd already had more than his fair share of good fortune. He'd tried his best and there could be no doubt that he'd given everything he possibly could, and made many sacrifices so that Shak might be a permanent success. But now he had to face the reality of failure and seek an alternative way of helping those unfortunate animals in most need. He switched out the lights as one of the bare bulbs flickered and popped because of its damp connection, and said goodnight to his dogs - which would soon need to be moved to a new home, wherever that might be.

Thirty

KENNEDY

The attack by Troy on Stephen looked like complicating even further the recent nosedive in Shak's fortunes. He lay in his hospital bed slowly regaining consciousness after heavy sedation, and could hear a clock ticking somewhere in the distance, and a tap dripping. Was it a tap? Although his eyes were closed he could tell there was a bright light shining overhead and in his dazed condition assumed it was the sun. He must've fallen asleep in the garden, he reasoned, and was very hungry - it felt like he hadn't eaten for days.

His thoughts drifted back to a week previously, when an elderly lady called Mary was walking her Yorkshire Terriers along a secluded path near her home. She could see a man ahead and didn't like the way he was behaving. He looked angry and impatient and launched a kick at the large, white and tan American Bulldog he held on a chain.

He was a young man, dressed in dirty denim with a thin, straggly beard. He held something in his right hand which at first Mary thought was a walking-stick, but it wasn't - it was something of similar proportions wrapped in a cloth. She hesitated and her stride faltered. The man saw her and stared.

'Oh dear,' she whispered to the terriers, concerned for her safety and theirs.

She stopped and was about to turn back, when the man strode towards her dragging the bulldog with him.

'Here,' he said loudly. 'If you like dogs take this fuckin' thing before I shoot it stone dead.'

She took the proffered chain and held it protectively to her chest, along with her own lead as she looked fearfully at the man, chin trembling slightly. He tucked the covered object under his stained jacket and hurried off along the path. Mary took all the dogs home, fed and watered them and telephoned the local authority, who in turn contacted Shak.

Stephen suddenly remembered he was partway through re-socialising the bulldog, re-named Kennedy because of the American connection, along with Troy and wondered why he was lying around in the garden on such a sunny day. He opened his eyes but the sun was blinding. He tried to move but seemed to be held down or entangled in some type of tubing.

'What the hell is going on?' he asked out loud.

Shadows moved overhead and he heard a distinctly Australian voice say: 'Hello Stephen, I'm Doctor Brugier and I'm looking after you. Do you know where you are right now?'

'Yes, I'm in the garden, what're you doing here doctor?'

'The garden? Right, well actually you've had a bit of an accident and you're in hospital. You have some serious injuries and are under sedation, so the medication is probably affecting your memory.'

'What, what happened? Was it a car-crash? Were Rachel and Neve with me?'

'They're all fine Stephen and no, it wasn't a car-crash - you were attacked by a dog.'

And then it started coming back to him. Doctor Brugier moved the spotlight and said, 'You've been in shock and that might've pushed the attack from your immediate memory as a coping mechanism.'

Stephen looked down at his prostrate body, and saw the dozens of stitches holding together his flesh in various places, with small tubes poking out here and there.

'We're still draining seroma and any infection,' explained the surgeon, nodding at the tubing. 'But you seem a lot better today and your temperature's stabilised.'

'Thank you for looking after me doctor, but I need to get back to work now.'

'I don't think you'll be up to doing much for a few days yet, but if you continue to improve you should be alright to continue recuperation at home by Monday.'

His recovery was hastened by a visit from an ambulance paramedic called William who said cheerfully, 'Hello Stephen, heard you were in here so thought I'd pop along and show you these pics of Bruce. You remember the big tan cross I got from you a few years ago?'

'Oh hi Will,' Stephen replied, squinting through his chemical haze at a vaguely familiar face.

'Here, have a look,' continued Will, holding up his telephone screen. 'He gets on really well with everybody and never shows any aggression at all, even though the guy at the council shelter said he would.'

'That's great,' said Stephen, focusing on a large dog cavorting around with William's children in their garden. 'You'll have years of happy times together and seeing him playing like that after nearly getting the needle, reminds me why I have to get my ass up and out of here as soon as possible.'

On Monday Stephen was back at the sanctuary feeling very stiff and slightly groggy, and a little more cautious around Kennedy and the other American Bulldogs.

'Can't believe Troy's actually gone,' he said softly, staring into an empty pen.

There was a silent pause before Rachel offered, 'We all thought it best to go with the vet's advice; there didn't seem to be any other choice at the time but at least it was done humanely and gently.'

'So sad, I was really getting somewhere with him.'

Rachel smiled and shook her head at Stephen's obstinate courage and dedication. He immediately pushed the dangers from his mind and carried on working, but Troy stayed forever in his memory with regret, as the one he let down.

Kennedy and new friend Layla

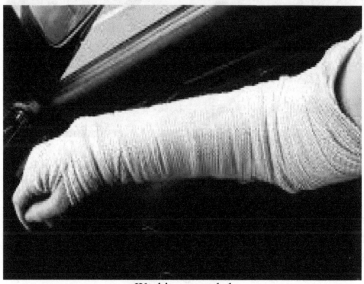

Working wounded

Thirty One

NANCY

Stephen was trying to come to terms with Troy's loss and the apparently unavoidable fact that Shak would soon no longer exist, or at best survive as a much smaller version of itself. Despite those depressing thoughts he continued to care for his dogs, and made a special point of taking as many as possible out to enjoy what time they had left together, sometimes in groups with Rachel and Neve up into the hills, or down to the beach and occasionally out into the wider community.

He got a call late one evening from out-of-hours responder John, saying that a Staffordshire Bull Terrier bitch had been picked up off the street where she'd been abandoned, and was being kennelled overnight by the council. The problem was that the dog had a large growth to her underside which would make her very difficult to re-home if the owners didn't come forward.

'And they probably won't,' John added. 'Because sorting out this lump is going to be expensive.'

'I hear what you're saying John,' Stephen replied. 'But to be honest we're totally full at the moment.'

'You mean you won't take her?'

'It's not that I won't, it's that I just don't have any room,' he replied, still not ready to admit the plight of his charity to anyone but himself.

There was a pregnant pause as John came to terms with the first refusal he'd ever heard Stephen make regarding the acceptance of a dog in need, before saying, 'Alright, I'll tell the council you can't take her.'

'Look, let's see if the owner comes forward first and take it from there.'

'I'll pass your message on.'

Stephen immediately felt guilty and sorrowful that he'd as good as refused to help a desperate dog, and his mind wrestled with the problem all night. The following day he received a follow-up call from Animal Welfare Officer, Neil:

'Hi Stephen, I'm just checking that I've got the facts right about the Staffie we took in last night - her owner hasn't come forward but I'm told you won't take her - is that correct?'

'It's not that I won't take her, Neil, it's that I can't. We have absolutely no room and to be honest…our finances are in such a bad state that I'm not sure we can carry on much longer.'

He'd finally said it out loud, and felt suddenly less burdened by the massive responsibility he was carrying around on his weary shoulders.

'Oh right, I'd no idea things were so desperate. It doesn't look too good for her then, unfortunately.'

Saddened by his friend's last remark, and feeling less pushed into a corner by the situation after admitting to current problems, he said, 'I'll tell you what Neil, have a look around and see if you can find somewhere else for her, and then you decide if she needs to come here or not?'

'Okay I can do that. I'll also take a good look at her myself first and let you know what I think her prospects are health-wise.'

Realising he'd just placed the pressure firmly back on himself, he felt depressed by the position he'd been forced into and began to doubt himself, his motives and everything he thought he'd achieved so far. Even if the Staffie bitch could be placed somewhere else, her condition and ubiquitous breed would make it almost impossible to re-home her quickly, making it just about certain that she'd be put to sleep within a few short weeks if not days.

He climbed into the truck, let his troubled head fall back and closed his eyes. Within minutes he was in a fitful, exhausted sleep which was tortured by a dream about the dogs he'd been forced to watch being killed by lethal injection, all those years ago at the Newcastle shelter.

After what seemed like a few minutes but was actually over an hour, a text message buzzed into his phone and throbbed in his pocket. He jerked awake and grabbed it in reflex, nightmarish scenes of persecuted, dying dogs still whirring around in his head, to read the following:

Hi Stephen, I have checked the dog over and she is in bad shape. No idea whether she can be treated successfully but the lump is the size of a grapefruit.

The breath caught in Stephen's throat as he read the message and for a moment, he almost gave way to the thought that all was lost anyway - so what was the point in worrying about it? But then he took control of himself and the situation, and realised that his overriding emotion was relief. Not relief that he didn't have to worry about this particular dog anymore - but relief that he might still have a second chance to save her. He texted back:

Bring her here right away.

Nancy had a very friendly, trustful nature like most Staffies and she got along with everybody. The growth to her underside was truly horrific though and required immediate attention. After agreeing a financial contribution to the treatment from the council, Stephen booked her into Moorview for x-rays and a fine-needle aspiration biopsy. The sample confirmed the lump as a malignant mammary tumour, but the x-rays indicated that no visible spread had occurred and she was re-booked for a complete excision. The operation was carried out successfully by surgeon, Alison at the Backworth referral clinic, who achieved reasonable margins around the mass and Nancy was discharged the following day.

It wasn't feasible for Nancy to be returned to the damp, muddy kennels to recover from surgery and avoid post-operative infection, so as he'd done so many times in the past, Stephen took her home. It increased the workload for him and Rachel, who with her daughter had eventually moved in permanently, but at least they could ensure full recovery.

Nancy settled in well to her new but temporary home, and got along well with the other eight dogs in residence. She recovered quickly and was soon running about the yard to burn up some of her endless energy, and maintain her terrier spirit. Her progress was gratifying to Stephen because he'd nearly let her go, which inspired him to carry on doing his best for all the dogs in his care.

He'd certainly never envisioned her lying in his lounge at any point when he got that first telephone call from John, yet there she was with the others and every time he looked at her it reminded him just how close he'd come to making a very bad decision, based purely on practicalities instead of conscience. He would certainly not let her down now and just in case her stitches were nipped by one of the other dogs whilst playing, he began taking her to work with him in the truck.

He also began stopping off for a drink at the Shoulder of Mutton pub in Longhorsley, named by a sheep-dependent community in pre-vegetarian times, usually in the company of long-time volunteers Michael and Alison on their way home from work on Fridays. He only ever had a slow one and classed it as therapy for himself, as the couple were a real tonic to be around, not least because of Michael's subtle humour which Stephen first noted during a hospital visit. Michael had been taken in after an injury to his arm, but was sitting cheerfully with it wrapped up tightly and a few painkillers in his bloodstream.

'Will you be able to manage alright at home when they let you out?' Stephen asked with concern.

'Well, there is one serious problem we can't see a way around,' Michael answered, looking despondently at his bandaged limb.

'Oh really, what's that?'

'Well, Alison's worried about who's going to pour her wine without spilling it when she's had a couple too many!'

They laughed until a nurse came to warn them of the possible consequences of the patient becoming too animated in his medicated condition.

'Okay, we'll cut down on the laughter,' Michael reassured her. 'But on a serious note - do you think I'll be able to play the piano when the bandages come off?'

'Oh, yes of course you will.'

'Well that's a bonus 'cause I couldn't play it before they went on!'

One Friday when Nancy was feeling particularly perky, the three amigos took her into the Shoulder with them. The pub was about half-full with leftover lunchtime customers who'd decided to stay for the afternoon shift, and early evening drinkers, mostly over-50s who didn't relish late-night revelling in crowded bars anymore. Another volunteer, Paul was present and came over to join them as they chatted.

Nancy was excited at all the people and noise, her unprofessionally-docked tail wagged wildly and she constantly pulled on her leash towards the nearest passing person. Most paused to pat and stroke her and ask about her still bandaged undercarriage, and she revelled in the attention.

Stephen bought a round which included a favourite Newcastle Brown Ale for Michael and a glass of house red for Alison, and they all sat in a circle dressed in scraped but still-muddy boots, stained and dog hair-covered work clothes, grasping their glasses with grubby hands. They were all tired after a hard day's graft and walking miles to exercise the many dogs, and Nancy managed to pull away from her tether towards two well-dressed ladies who were sitting opposite, sipping drinks and chatting. Stephen grabbed Nancy at the last moment before she broke free but one of the women said, 'It's alright, let her come over and say hello.'

'Are you sure, she's a bit boisterous?' Stephen asked.

'Yes she's fine, we love dogs, let her come.'

He did so and Nancy ran straight over, hopped up onto the sofa between the women and lay down.

'Oh she's lovely,' one said as they both patted and stroked her. 'Has she had an operation?'

Stephen told them all about the surgery and its complications but that her future prognosis was good.

'So is she your only dog?'

'No she's not - I have just over sixty at the moment,' he replied with a straight face.

'Sixty!?'

'Yeah, sixty-three altogether if I remember correctly,' he answered as the others burst into laughter.

He then went on to explain all about Shak and the blonde lady who said her name was Kerry, asked, 'So yours is the only charity in the whole country which accepts dogs that would otherwise be put to sleep?'

'As far as we know.'

'Well that's really interesting and what a coincidence because as I say, I love dogs and I retired early from work recently, so I'm looking for something to occupy my time.'

Stephen gave her a card with contact details, and the two women got up to leave shortly afterwards, saying goodbye and handing Nancy over with some regret.

'Bye,' Stephen replied. 'Hope to hear from you, we always need reliable volunteers.'

'Well my husband and I are off on holiday for a few weeks soon but I'll be in touch when we get back.'

They left and as the door swung shut behind them, Michael took a gulp of his ale and said, 'No way will they show up at the kennels, not more than once anyway after they've snapped a heel or splashed dog shite on one of those expensive handbags.'

They all laughed again and nodded in agreement, but Stephen's returning faith and optimism caused him to ponder, 'You never know though, she sounded serious and stranger things have happened.'

As Nancy continued to recover and improve, Michael and Alison took her out walking daily and inevitably fell in love with her. When Lexi, another Shak dog they'd cared for, sadly died after many happy years with them, they adopted Nancy and took her home to enjoy her remaining time there too.

Thirty Two

EMBER

Just after Nancy left Stephen received a phone call one day as he and David dragged a cage through the kennel mud. Recognising Gemma's number, an Animal Welfare Officer who had previously worked part-time for Shak as an out-of-hours responder, he told David to take a break and answered.

'I need a huge favour if you can possibly manage it, Stephen?'

'Oh yeah?' he replied, kicking some of the clinging mud from his boots and clumping into the cabin.

'Yes, I have a dog that I've just pulled off the street and she's emaciated with skin problems as well.'

'Okay,' Stephen said, filling the battered kettle with his free hand. 'What is it, another thrown away Staffie?'

'No, she's a little bigger.'

'Oh?'

'Uh-hum, she's a Dog de Bordeaux.'

'Wow, that's a big, powerful animal, Gemma.'

'She's quiet as a mouse though Stephen, and she's in a bad way and needs your help.'

'I'm sure I can do something but we've been kind of running the operation down just lately.'

'I heard something about that but was told things were looking a little brighter recently?'

'Mm, maybe but to be honest I have zero experience with that breed. I had minimal contact with one at the RSPCA shelter but that's all.'

'She's just another innocent dog in dire need, Stephen, and she needs the help only you can give her right now because I'm not going to be able to keep her alive for very long otherwise.'

Stephen paused and remembered how close he'd come to rejecting Nancy, and Gemma took advantage of the silence: 'She was reported as found by a local bloke who took her in, and was lying on his sofa in front of the fire when I got there.'

'She must've had a home somewhere before then, and was just thrown out on the street?'

'Looks like it, or the guy just couldn't be bothered anymore because of her skin and a lump she has on the side of her face.'

'Not a lot going for her then?'

'No, she seems calm around people and other dogs but is very thin and depressed.'

'It'll take some work but I could maybe have a look at her?'

'Good because we have to at least try, don't we? That's what you always told me - the day you stop trying to save them all is the day you might as well pack it in?'

He smiled to himself at the little dig, but respected Gemma's opinions because she'd proved herself so often in the past. She pursued animal abusers without mercy and even persuaded the council into initiating prosecutions for the first time in years.

'So you'll take a look and see what you think her prospects are?'

'I'll take a look because it's you who's asking, but I can't promise anything because we haven't got any room for her here.'

He poured boiling water from the kettle into a grimy mug containing a used tea bag, and called the staff over to inform them of the situation. 'It's going to be difficult for all of us if we take this one in because of her size, her condition and her untested character, as well as our lack of space.'

Without any conversation they all agreed immediately: 'Bring her in, we can handle it,' was the general reply. 'We nearly said no to Nancy and look how well she turned out,' added Michael.

She arrived that evening because there was little time to spare before she ended up on the kill-list, and was put in a pen where she sat silently. She looked totally miserable, hardly moved and wouldn't eat. A vet appointment was booked and she was checked over, tests were done and skin-scrapes taken, and medication prescribed. On examination, the lump to her face was found to be just a bony mass that required no action. Her skin began to clear after a few weeks' treatment and she began to nibble at her food, but not enough to put any weight on her rangy frame.

Because she was so weak and miserable in the kennels environment, Stephen took her home with him, 'Just for a few days,' he told Rachel, and also put her in the truck when he drove to and from work.

'She should have a name now she's decided to hang around and stay with us,' Rachel suggested one evening during a rare restaurant meal with friends.

'So what should we call her?' he asked.

'Well, I was just thinking about that. She's kind of a reddish colour and sparked back when we all thought the light was going out forever, but there was still a flickering ember of life left in her.'

'Yeah?'

'So let's call her Ember?'

'Good idea, Ember it is.'

At last she began to perk up and put on a little weight, and a few months later a suitable foster home was found. Just before Christmas 2016 though her health nosedived, she lost her appetite altogether and rapidly began to lose all the weight she'd gained. She was returned to the vet but no clear cause for her decline could be identified, and Stephen felt certain she'd finally given up altogether and was preparing to die. He advised the prospective fosterers that taking her in that condition would not be fair to them, and took her home to spend her last days in peace and comfort.

Although Stephen was as busy as always over the Christmas holidays, the sick dog stayed home with Rachel and Grace. Neve and various others came to visit and all showed caring concern for the poor, wasted animal. Slowly, in that warm, safe and positive environment she began to take an interest and perked up; eventually resumed eating and her general health improved considerably. The more she rallied the more she was encouraged, and was soon going for short walks around the yard. After that her recovery accelerated and she resumed her place in Stephen's truck every day, and he decided against fostering her out.

Her skin complaint cleared up although discoloured patches were still visible, and Stephen started taking her into the Shoulder with him on Friday visits. She was very relaxed around people and soon became friends with all the regular customers. Most were shocked at her still very thin condition, and amazed that she'd retained any tolerance at all for the species which had caused her so much suffering. Many asked about her abandonment, future prospects and also about Shak.

She became very popular and some regulars adjusted their visiting times to coincide with hers, so they could take her for little walks around the bar or out into the beer-garden. Without pushing things at any point, Stephen used every opportunity to talk about his charity and its aims, and found that his enthusiasm for it had returned as he'd helped life return to Ember, after she almost gave up as well.

He was shovelling shit one morning as the rest of the team took dogs out for the first of two daily walks, and moved in to clean each pen as it was vacated. There were other things he could've been doing but he never asked his staff to do anything he wasn't prepared to do himself.

His phone buzzed to tell him he had a message and he was tempted to ignore it, but then leant the square-mouth shovel against the cage bars, peeled off his sodden gloves and fished out the phone. At first he didn't recognise the sender but then realised it was the blonde woman who'd taken such an interest in Nancy a few weeks back. She was coming home from her extended holiday and still keen to volunteer at the kennels, and added a little background information including the fact that she'd worked as a secretary for many years.

That could be useful, he thought, recalling the pile of untended paperwork waiting at home for him, and arranged to meet her at the Shoulder for an initial chat when she got back.

Thirty Three

PROGRESS

'If she does agree to help with the paperwork she'll need somewhere to do it. You can't expect her to sit at home with it while she's eating her tea, like you do,' Joan advised Stephen when he told her about the prospective new volunteer.

'What about here in the cabin?'

'No, she won't stay in here for five minutes and anyway, I've been talking with some of the other volunteers and we all think Shak needs some kind of interior space we could use for more organised fundraising, like selling tee-shirts, hats, books, prints and anything else we can think of.'

'Sounds like a good idea but...' Stephen replied, looking out across the sea of winter mud in the kennels.

'No I wasn't thinking of out there either, there isn't enough room for the dogs never mind market stalls.'

'Where then?'

'I was thinking we could perhaps look out for somewhere cheap to rent, which would pay for itself and a bit more besides.'

Stephen paused to think awhile. 'It's a good idea mam but I don't think we can afford it.'

'We just need to stay afloat until it gets off the ground, and we'll start advertising right away. You could also give some of your educational talks to get as many people as possible interested?'

'Yeah I could do that, and maybe get some others to do talks and demonstrations as well.'

They trawled through the local papers and eventually spoke to an estate agent, who suggested a currently vacant property on Greenwell Road, Alnwick. The premises were spacious considering the reasonable rent, particularly in expensive Alnwick, and they immediately liked the upper floor.

'There's plenty room up here for stalls and even permanent displays,' said Joan, walking around the area. 'After a good clean that is.'

'We can all help with that,' offered her son. 'And you're right - we could have racks and displays on the walls, and a nice big desk up at the far end in front of the windows by the radiator!'

'Yes, so it would be like a separate office space where the paperwork could be done. Can we afford it?'

'I think we could scrape enough together for the first month, but we'd have to get some money coming in from it as soon as possible.'

'Well let's tell the estate agent bloke we'll take it before anybody else steps in, and get cracking straight away.'

They moved in a fortnight later, cleaned the place and furnished it from donations and second-hand clearance sales. Joan and her team did some research and preparation, and got off to a flying start with a 3-day Shak Boutique sale of donated clothes and household goods, run by Jill who still operated their Facebook page. This was followed by the formation of Santa's Helpers to collect Christmas donations phoned in by the public, and the new Shak Headquarters was soon off and running successfully.

For the first time in many months Stephen and all the Shak helpers began to feel the return of a little stability, and were able to interact far more with the community from their new base. Stephen ran a series of talks; his friends from Moorview Vets did some seminars and various supportive experts volunteered their services in displays of canine behaviour, alternative health therapies and dietary advice. Regular volunteering information days were held to explain requirements, rewards and possible pitfalls, and as a result more helpers came forward and spread awareness of Shak even wider.

Kerry turned up on time at the Shoulder with husband Gordon, whose father had been a prominent Labour politician, and there wasn't a handbag in sight - maybe she left it in the car?

She'd told Gordon all about Shak and he ordered drinks for all the staff and volunteers present, in recognition of their hard work. She sat down across a table from Stephen and told him she'd like to walk dogs as much as she could manage, because she wanted to interact directly with them and it would provide exercise for her at the same time.

'That's fine,' he said, keeping in mind how many people had shown similar enthusiasm to begin with, only to lose it all a week later. 'Have you done anything like this before?'

'Not really. We've had dogs and still have cats, which I love but they don't need much walking.'

'No, probably not,' he smiled. 'So what else have you done?'

'Well as I said earlier, I worked as a secretary until quite recently.'

'Oh yes, I remember.'

'Yes, a solicitor's secretary.'

'Oh right, that could be useful.'

She briefly went through her past duties and Stephen quickly recognised that her administration and office skills could be essential to Shak, and take a lot of work off his shoulders.

'So when could you start?' he asked.

'I can start right away.'

The following Monday morning Stephen passed all the paperwork that had lain around on his makeshift desk at home for months, to Kerry at her new HQ position. He soon gave her full autonomy to make decisions and take appropriate actions on behalf of Shak, and immediately the pressure lifted as she swiftly caught up with the lengthy backlog of documentation. She then moved onto research fund-raising possibilities and squeezed in some dog walking as well. Stephen could hardly believe the sudden changes to his daily life and his spirits soared accordingly, but then his learned wariness returned as he remembered people he'd placed hope and trust in before,

211

only to be let down badly when they fully realised the amount of unrelenting work involved.

Despite the constant flow of paperwork that required attention, Kerry kept her feet firmly grounded and used them to walk the Shak dogs as often as possible, always with her *fitbit* strapped to a wrist. So she kept in touch with both sides of the charity and knew exactly how important each was to the other, and was very good at balancing the two. Soon she was organising various events in addition to Joan's relentless fundraising, including a big charity night at the Shoulder which was a huge success. It all brought in additional funds and more people got on board in support of the unique charity based in their home area, and it seemed apparent that Kerry was a real grafter who wasn't going to back out anytime soon. The surge she initiated in the pub continued to roll forward as more and more local people pitched in following her example.

Ember realised that she now lived permanently in a stable, cruelty-free environment and grew from strength to strength, continuing to gain weight and shake off the sadness that had pervaded her mind for so long. Stephen sat sipping a cold beer one Friday in early spring 2017, as Ember entertained the Shoulder regulars by just looking happy and eating their treats. As he thought about the immense difference Kerry had already made to Shak and therefore to him, he remembered how he'd first met her. Perhaps in some strange, unexplained way little Nancy had repaid him for saving her life by introducing Kerry into his? A far-fetched notion, he admitted to himself as Ember turned to make sure he was still there with her, but a notion he was going to hang onto all the same.

Over the coming months Kerry helped spread the word about Shak amongst different sectors of the regional community, including some very well-heeled friends and associates of her and Gordon, himself a successful businessman and property owner. They introduced Stephen to Neil; proprietor of a very lucrative commercial vending machine operation. He was a dog-lover and passionate supporter of animal welfare generally, and they immediately struck up a friendship.

One evening as Stephen discussed Shak's financial position with Kerry, his phone rang and he picked up straight away as relief from the never-ending rows of figures on the sheets in front of him.

'Hello?' he answered brightly.

'Hello,' replied a quietly spoken female voice. 'Is this Shak?'

'Yes it is, can I help you?'

'Well, my name's Pauline - Pauline Bramley and my son Gary runs his own building company.'

'Oh yes?' Stephen replied, slightly puzzled but not perturbed.

'Yes and we're both very interested in animal charities.'

'Oh, right.'

'And we were wondering if there's any work you need doing?'

'Oh, well, yes there's always plenty of that, why, are you offering a decent discount?'

Thirty Four

BLADE

Blade

'So was that afternoon in the pub the first you'd heard of us?' Stephen asked Kerry one day as they worked on the detailed preparation of contracts for Shak staff.

'No, I had a friend who volunteered for a while and she often asked me to join her, but I was working long hours and travelling a lot with my job at the time.'

'Yeah, it can be a burden if you have a lot of other commitments.'

'I know, Gordon warned me I'd be taking too much on as well, but it was always in the back of my mind after I read about you in the papers and had a look at your website.'

'So how long ago was that?'

'Oh, years back but after I finally packed in working I was out at Whickham, celebrating with some old friends and my sister-in-law Jill one afternoon. Gordon picked us up and on the way home we called into the Shoulder because it's quite close to our house.'

'I know the place well,' Stephen smiled, putting a question mark against one of the new workers' rights he was signing up to but doubted he could afford.

Kerry laughed. 'Well fortunately, you were in there that very night with some friends and a beautiful little Staffie.'

'That'd be Paul, Michael and Alison with Nancy?'

'Yes but I didn't know any of you at the time. I stopped on my way to the bar to say hello to Nancy, and Michael told me she'd just come back from the vet after a major operation. The poor little mite had stitches the full length of her tummy but still seemed really bright and happy.'

'It was a tumour but she got through the surgery in good shape.'

'I know and when I sat down, to my amazement she trotted over and climbed up on the seat with me and Jill!'

'I remember that, and the look of surprise on your face; we half expected you to push her down.'

'No way, Jill hugged her and she clambered up on my knee and I gave her a big cuddle too, and you lot were all laughing.'

'Only because we were happy to see her making friends and enjoying herself, after her operation and everything.'

'I knew that, and I asked Michael how long they'd had her but he said just about an hour actually. I was a little confused but Alison said Nancy was a rescued dog who'd been living at the Shak kennels. I remembered the name and began asking questions about the charity. Alison said she and Michael were volunteers, then introduced you and said you were the founder.'

'I always feel a bit embarrassed when people say that, it always sounds a bit too grand, don't you think?'

'No I don't and you should be very proud of what you've achieved.'

'Mm, I'll try harder but we still have a long way to go,' he smiled.

'Alison said they were taking Nancy home and hoping she'd settle in with them, so they could look after her for the rest of her life, and they seemed such nice people. They had two other Staffies from Shak, and another dog which had just died.'

'Yeah that was a shame. So how did I come across? Most people think I'm miserable 'cause I'm always talking about dogs who need help.'

'Only sometimes,' she laughed. 'Just joking but you were a bit more business-like which I'd expect from the *founder*,' she replied, emphasizing the last word.

He laughed as Kerry continued, 'I asked what volunteering at Shak was like and mentioned that I'd been interested for quite a while. Alison said volunteers have to be committed because the dogs need stability and continuity and familiar faces around them, so it was no good just popping in and out when it suits you - the dogs have to come first.'

217

'Which is true.'

'I know it is and my heart sank, because Gordon had also retired recently and was enjoying travelling and flying off to see family in Australia, or staying at our place in Menorca.'

'Yeah I remember you saying that.'

'I said I'd love to volunteer though and was willing to do absolutely anything, but would understand if it wasn't possible.'

'But you were going off somewhere pretty soon as I recall?'

'Yes, we were going to Menorca the following week for a few months, so you told me to send you an email with some background information, and saying what I'd like to do at Shak.'

'Oh yeah, I remember the email now - very impressive!'

'I didn't think so and didn't think I'd be any use to you because of all the time away, but you replied and asked me to get in touch when I got back. So I did exactly that and we met for a chat, and I began my first day at Shak the following Monday.'

'And the rest as they say - is history!'

'It is now but I was very nervous when I pulled up alongside Alison and Michael, who'd arrived at the kennels just before me. Apart from our family mongrel, Albert, I hadn't had much to do with dogs so was relieved at seeing someone I knew a little. As we walked into the kennels my knees went weak at the howling and barking from fifty something dogs, and also the overpowering smell. I'd never heard or smelled anything like it and thought in panic, what on earth have I done?'

Stephen laughed and said, 'It can be a bit much to take in first time around, but you soon get used to it.'

'Right at that point I wasn't sure I wanted to get used to it but I was ushered into a little cabin and introduced to Rachel for the first time. She was lovely and gave me some basic instructions, and my first day at Shak was under way.'

'So how'd it go?'

'Well I grabbed a bucket, two brushes, poop bags, clean bedding and off I went in search of Alison again. She showed me how to thoroughly clean each kennel as soon as it was vacated, before the resident dog came back from being walked or moved. It was strictly one cleaner to one kennel though and I was terrified on my own as most of the nearby dogs were huge, but as time passed I realised they were just as terrified of me.'

Stephen nodded and was interested in what Kerry was saying. 'Go on,' he encouraged her.

'Well I'm not particularly a terrifying person most of the time so it struck me just how much those poor animals must have suffered at the hands of horrid people. Those thoughts made me even more determined to help them and I scrubbed as fast and as hard as ever in my life. I don't wash many floors nowadays but certainly never considered myself above hard, physical work.'

'No, that wouldn't have worked out so well for us.'

'Michael moved the dogs around to empty each kennel for cleaning and we got through them surprisingly quickly. Alison said we'd be able to walk some of them when we finished, so I looked forward to that.'

'Was I there that day?'

'Yes, you were whizzing around and looking after the difficult cases, and I was told not to go near because they can be really heartbreaking.'

'Right.'

'There were other staff and volunteers working but I just stayed close to Alison.'

'She and Michael definitely know the ropes and have been giving up their time to help the dogs for years.'

'They're good at it as well and after lunch Michael said I could walk a Lurcher called Fagan. He put him on a leash and took us out front, and I was nervous again but didn't have to be - all Fagan wanted was a long walk and a big cuddle at the end of it! We became friends that day and I look forward to seeing his handsome face as often as I can.'

'He's a good boy. We never have trouble with the Lurchers as long as we don't let them loose in the open fields. They're sight-hunters and could end up literally miles away chasing a butterfly or something!'

'They're lovely and my next walk was with another Lurcher called Corbyn.'

'We named him after Jeremy because he's very laid-back but wants to do everything his way.'

They both laughed and Kerry said, 'He's definitely laid-back, in fact he'll lie down and let you stroke his tummy all day if you've got the time!'

'Yeah, he came in with two pals - Boris and Nigel and I bet Boris would like his belly stroked as well!'

'Not too sure about Nigel though, he's always trying to break free and might just snap your fingers off!'

They both laughed again before Kerry said, 'Actually that reminds me of little Chuck the Staffie, not that they look much alike.'

'Maybe Boris a little?' Stephen suggested to another burst of laughter.

'Poor Chuck, is it true he's called that because he was chucked out of a moving car?'

'It was a van - I got an out-of-hours call on the way to the Metro Centre with Rachel and Grace. We were going to buy presents for Neve's birthday, and the call collection was way up at Lynemouth.'

'Oh, so it was you who picked him up?'

'Yes, we were already down the A1 as far as Stannington, but I was told by the council it was an emergency so I turned around at the junction there and drove back up. When we arrived I spoke to the family who'd reported the dog, and they were eye-witnesses.'

'So what actually happened?'

'The family live on the corner of a terrace with a lane behind it, and the woman was at the kitchen window in the back, washing dishes. She said a white Transit van pulled around the corner into the lane, the passenger door opened and Chuck came flying out, and the van sped off without even slowing down.'

'Oh my God it's a wonder the little chap's still alive.'

'It's amazing but he was hardly hurt at all. I checked him over, put him in the truck with Rachel and Grace and we took him shopping with us!'

'He's a lucky boy. He scared the life out of me at first though because he likes to play with his lead and grabs at it when he's out walking, and I thought he was trying to bite me!'

'No, we'd never let you take a dangerous dog out - that's my department. You get them when I've sorted out their defensive aggression and they're reasonably calm again.'

'I know that now but I didn't then. All he wants to do is play with his lead, eat treats and have his tummy tickled. It breaks my heart to think of what happened to him because he just wants to be with people all the time. He gets into scrapes with other dogs because he's so desperate to play, but like so many of us - his intentions are often misunderstood!'

'You're right there - sometimes I don't even understand myself!'

'You left before lunch to take one of the dogs to the vet that day, but came back in the afternoon and we had another chat, and that's when you asked if I'd be interested in helping out with the admin' work as you were falling behind with it.'

'I just didn't have the time and was becoming inundated with it all. It got so bad I'd started to ignore it but I knew it wouldn't go away.'

'No it definitely hadn't gone away so I agreed to do one day at the kennels and one day trying to get the paperwork under control.'

'And I'm eternally grateful that you eventually did,' he smiled.

'I still want to work with the dogs though Stephen, because although Chuck's story broke my heart, I was even more saddened and shocked later that afternoon when I got back from walking him, and saw the dog warden's van parked outside.'

'Was that when Blade came in?'

'Yes, I went inside and saw you, Rachel and Gemma the warden huddled around a dog lying on the floor. At first I thought it was dead but after I re-kennelled Chuck, I went over to see a bedraggled, semi-collapsed German Shepherd panting like mad, do you remember?'

'Only too well, we nearly lost poor Blade there and then but managed to bring him around. He had a serious skin infection plus flea-allergy, and open wounds where his too-tight collar had bitten into him for months if not years. He also had infection in both ears and CDRM affecting his back legs.'

'What a state he was in; he could hardly stand. Why do so many Shepherds get that particular problem?'

'Because of stupid fads and fancies of ignorant breeders. Shepherds backs are not supposed to slope down to their hind legs. If you look at photographs from the early twentieth century they're completely straight and level across their backs.'

'I've heard that for a dog to be healthy its shape should resemble that of a wolf as much as possible, as that's where they all originated?'

Stephen didn't answer, apparently doubtful.

'There are a lot of breeds with genetic problems nowadays I believe?' Kerry continued.

'Yes but Blade's overall condition was a bloody disgrace, once again. So often dogs have been in a home environment but are totally neglected and abused, and are signed over by the monsters who *own* them to be destroyed because they can't be bothered anymore.'

'Oh no, don't Stephen, you're making me cry again just thinking about him.'

'It doesn't make me cry anymore, Kerry. I've seen it and even worse so many times now it makes me want to scream in anger and frustration. People who use the word sentimental about dog-lovers obviously have no idea what we're talking about.'

They paused for a minute, remembering the innocent dog who'd suffered so much and stayed in both their hearts, and Kerry said softly, 'He let me stroke him even though his skin was torturing him, and I will never forget the look in his eyes. I have never seen such sad hopelessness.'

They paused again, both contemplating the horrendous cruelty so many animals suffer at the hands of unworthy people, and knowing for certain why they worked at Shak.

'A few days later you let me help bathe him, do you remember?'

Stephen nodded, still remembering the terrible traumas he'd witnessed over the years.

'You were so gentle with him and he knew you were trying to help him,' Kerry continued. 'It was probably the first time in his life anyone ever had, but his skin was in such bad condition that it started to bleed.'

'So did my heart.'

Kerry paused for another silent moment before asking, 'Were you with him at the end?'

'Yes, he was panting hard again that Wednesday so I took him to the vet. He was very lethargic and wouldn't eat so Moorview squeezed him in, but x-rays couldn't pinpoint what was making him ill and after 3 days of intravenous fluids and antibiotics, his temperature was still extremely high. I was called by Moorview on Friday afternoon as he was very weak; his back legs had gone altogether, and they were still baffled as to what was causing it all. I spent an hour with him which is so precious to me now. He still knew who I was and also recognised Paul, who went with me. I got into his kennel and hugged him, and he looked so frail and sad that I didn't want to leave.

After speaking with Vio and Frankie - the vet and nurse who were looking after him, it was obvious that we only had two choices - let him go there and then or risk general anaesthetic for a CT scan to try and find out what the problem was. Paul and I agreed that we weren't giving up on him without doing everything we could, so authorised the scans. They provided answers but not the ones we'd hoped for. Poor Blade's liver and kidneys were inflamed and enlarged, and both were covered in cysts and tumours, all probably a result of the poor care and diet he'd received all his miserable life. Curative treatment wasn't possible so we sat with him again and hoped for some miraculous improvement.

We were called out to another case but about seven o'clock that evening I got a call saying Blade was gasping and deteriorating rapidly, so I dropped everything and rushed to be with him. I arrived to find his head cradled in Frankie's lap and I took over from her. He was dying there in front of us and beautiful Blade finally left this cruel world nuzzling into me so peacefully and calmly, after his desperate attempts to stay with us.'

Stephen paused and gazed into space. Kerry stayed silent.

'Blade had an awful existence before he came to us, yet he was such a gentleman and brave character that it feels like he was with us for a lot longer than the short time he actually was. I loved him dearly as did everyone who tried so hard to help him, and he'll be missed always. I'll never forget how pleased he was to be with us, and being able to make him happy for a little while at least is something I'll forever be grateful for.'

Thirty Five

PLANS

'**W**ell things certainly seem a bit brighter around here,' said Joan as she parked her handbag on the edge of the recycled desk by the window. 'How are you settling in, Kerry?'

'I'm fine thank you Joan, how are you?'

'I'd been looking forward to a nice relaxing retirement but it looks like I'll have to postpone that for a while.'

'You should retire if you want to, mam,' said Stephen who was busy carrying boxes full of various items up the steep stairs. 'But I bet it wouldn't last a week before you'd be back here looking for something to do!'

They all laughed and at that moment Stephen's mobile rang from a number he didn't recognise.

'Hello?' he answered warily, hoping it wasn't a member of the public with another stray dog.

'Oh hello,' replied a vaguely familiar voice. 'It's Pauline again - Pauline Bramley. I'm just making sure you haven't forgotten our meeting this afternoon? I know how busy you are.'

'Oh er no, I hadn't forgotten,' he lied. 'In fact I'm here already trying to clean the place up a bit for your visit. We had another sale at the weekend.'

'Oh good, hope it went well. I'll be with you soon then.'

The three colleagues managed to clear the floor of boxes and sales debris, and the two women sat Stephen down at the desk, fussing around it to make him look as official as possible with pen in hand, before the doorbell rang. Kerry answered it and escorted Mrs Bramley upstairs.

'Well you see,' she said, settling into the recently repaired chair opposite Stephen. 'My son Gary has known about Shak for years and he asked me to track you down if I could.'

'Right, yes we haven't been here very long and don't give out the address of the kennels, because we'd be inundated with dogs that people don't want anymore.'

'Oh I see, yes I should've thought; we know you don't take strays in from the general public.'

'That's right, we normally just take in those that other rescue places won't, for one reason or another.'

'Yes, I think that's what caught Gary's interest in the first place.'

'Oh good,' Stephen said, wondering where the conversation was going but not wanting to rush it or appear rude.

'So you're probably wondering why I'm here?'

'Well I remember you said something about building work?'

'Yes that's right. Gary owns a building company - Davison Contracts, and we're also very interested in animal welfare.'

'That's good of you; animals need all the help they can get.'

'I can imagine,' she replied, glancing quickly around the room and smiling at Joan and Kerry, who were discreetly replenishing racks and hooks with items of clothing. 'And we like to support worthy charities as much as possible.'

'Good, as I say…'

'I don't just mean by handing over cash though.'

'Oh?'

'No, we like to provide help in the form of building works, but it has to be something that directly improves the animals' lives.'

'Right, well just about anything will do that in our case.'

'So you have some building work requirements which fit that category?'

'Oh yes, definitely, we have lots of things that need doing which will improve all our lives.'

'You realise we'd have to visit the kennels first to assess the work?'

'Yes, obviously, I can arrange that. How much work are we talking about Mrs Bramley because we have any amount of small repairs?'

'Gary and my husband John will tell you how much they can do for you, once they've had a look around the place and please, call me Pauline.'

'Alright Pauline, how soon would they like to visit?'

'They're just finishing a previous project at another charity, but will want to start as soon as possible before the better weather gets here and things begin to take off generally again.'

It was very cold and bleak outside when Gary and John arrived at the kennels a few days later, and much the same inside. The two builders had a brief chat with Stephen in the cabin, as they glanced critically around the flimsy structure before stepping out into the semi-frozen mud.

'The first thing you need,' announced John, hands deep in pockets with a miserable frown on his face. 'Is a proper concrete floor with adequate drainage.'

'A floor with drainage?' repeated Stephen who'd been thinking more along the lines of a repaired hinge here and there. 'Do you do that kind of thing?'

'Sometimes, it all depends on the individual situation,' Gary answered, walking across to the pens to say hello to the dogs, who all barked frantically in reply.

John's frown deepened at the increased noise and he walked towards the exit. Stephen assumed he was leaving in disgust but he stopped near the main door, turned and looked back into the kennel space. 'You've obviously run out of room,' he suggested, nodding at the large central runs. 'Do you really need those six big cages right in the middle?'

'Erm, they're what we call the runs and we put the dogs in there so we can clean their pens out. We've got some living in there at the moment because we're out of kennel space as you noticed.'

'Right, but do the runs need to be that big?'

'I've er, I've never thought about it - that's the size they were when we got them.'

John turned to Gary and said, 'If we partition those six in half and put gates at both ends instead of just one, we'll have twelve pens instead of six right away.'

Stephen stood with his mouth slightly open, seeing the space in a whole new light. Gary nodded and said to him, 'John's got a pretty good eye for this kind of thing.'

'That's an absolutely brilliant idea - I can't think why it didn't occur to me before.'

'Because you're a dog rescuer and good at what you do, and we're professional builders and good at what we do.'

'Right, I'm fine with that but what will it all cost?' Stephen asked, hoping he wasn't right in the middle of being conned into a lot of expensive work.

'It won't cost you anything - we'll do it but don't keep pestering the lads with cups of tea,' John replied. 'It slows them down and I want this finished as soon as possible.'

'No problem,' Stephen choked. 'And thank you so much, I can hardly believe it!'

'So we'll call the floor with drainage and work to the pens - Phase One,' continued John.

'Phase One, you mean there's more?'

'And for Phase Two,' added Gary. 'We'll shift your shed and build a proper canteen with an office and kitchen attached.'

'Wow, honestly?'

'It'll be classed as temporary so it can be moved if need be, but will have plumbing and hot water on tap.'

'Hot water? Sounds like Heaven. It's starting to feel like I'm on Candid Camera and you're going to burst out laughing any minute and tell me you're joking.'

'No we're deadly serious,' intervened John. 'I'll check falls and angles for the drainage, draw some plans up, then work out a budget and programme - which will be tight because I don't want to be here one minute longer than I have to be.'

'Have you a lot of other work on?'

'Not particularly but it's cold, wet and very noisy in here, and it stinks so we won't be hanging around.'

Stephen considered saying that they would get used to the smell, everybody did, but decided against it, thanked the two men again and asked when they'd like to start the work.

'Just off the top of my head I'd say six men and some machinery for six weeks for Phase One, so how soon can you move the dogs out of the centre pens?'

'Move them out? I've nowhere to move them to.'

Thirty Six

GROUNDWORKS

'Well we can't do anything with the dogs and runs still in place,' said John, sweeping his hand in a semi-circle.

'No, obviously not but don't worry,' Stephen replied after a thoughtful pause. 'I'll have them shifted by the start date.'

Finding accommodation for 16 dogs for 6 weeks could have been a daunting task but luckily George, who runs a boarding kennel not too far away, said he could find enough room on one condition - which was that Stephen supplied assistance to look after them. He got in touch with Susan who had volunteered for Shak previously, and just by chance had recently finished working at a grooming parlour.

'Any chance you might help us out 'til you find another job?' he asked hopefully.

'Well, I suppose it'll keep me busy but I might have to leave you in the lurch as soon as something turns up.'

'Any help will be great because I know you can handle it on your own. Obviously you'll have to leave us sometime but it's only for six weeks in all and is a bit of an emergency.'

She started the following week and they began by moving the dogs out and into their temporary home, a few miles south. The transfer went smoothly but Stephen was constantly worried about building work at Shak not starting on time, because that would mean more rent due to George - if he still had room for the extra weeks. He'd heard all the old tales about builders and wondered if they'd even turn up at all, given the fact that they weren't being paid for the job.

His doubts proved unfounded though as they arrived early on the arranged date, and started work straight away. They'd obviously been fully briefed and marched in with confident intent, carrying an assortment of tools and equipment. They dismantled the metalwork and cleared the whole central area before lunchtime.

There were plenty of jokes and good-natured banter amongst the men which created a vibrant, sociable atmosphere. They never interfered with Shak staff or went near any of the remaining dogs, which seemed to pick up on the positive activity and weren't at all disturbed by all the coming and going, cheerful singing and shouting, or even the accompanying banging, crashing, sawing and drilling.

The dogs all peered through their bars when the builders arrived each morning. They were obviously interested and in turn - the builders began to show interest in them. During breaks they would often walk around sipping tea or coffee and talking to them, without getting too close, and eventually began asking questions about different animals including their conditions and treatments. Everybody got to know each other and the visitors were actually a pleasure to have around.

One afternoon a very defensive Akita-cross was brought in, and the crew stopped work to watch it being unloaded and penned with the use of rigid-leashes. The chunky, Japanese fighting-breed male had been chained to a lamp-post and abandoned, and didn't trust anybody.

They guys gathered around as Stephen used his litter-tongs to slowly remove the heavy chain from around the dog's neck, whilst keeping his distance outside the cage. The chain must have been very uncomfortable for the dog because it realised straight away that Stephen was trying to help it, and calmed down from the tugging, lunging and dangerous animal it had been on arrival.

John in particular took an interest in Yoshi after that day; made a point of saying hello to him every morning, and began to understand why every dog is worth the effort of saving from abuse and execution.

After the area was cleared, hard-cored and open, free-running drains were plotted so the pens could be washed out straight into them, John called in plant-hire company D.A. Johnstone who also gave their time and effort for nothing. They brought a wheeled excavator to demolish the old walkways and cattle troughs around the inner perimeter, with an attached pneumatic breaker which was extremely and unrelentingly noisy. Conditions became more testing for the Shak staff but they all carried on regardless and remained positive about the work, which they knew was necessary to improve every aspect of the charity.

One of the builders, Ryan who was working on the drainage, asked Stephen about Lady, a bulldog kennelled nearby who looked at him with a sad expression.

'She was badly abused,' Stephen replied. 'She came in quite recently and was very scared and I thought we'd need a long time to bring her around, but with you for company every day she's doing well!'

'Yeah?'

'Yeah, you show her respect so she's accepted you.'

Ryan smiled and looked back at Lady.

'In fact I think she might even like you,' Stephen added with a grin.

'That's most likely because I give her half my sandwiches every day - my mam says I'm losing weight!'

The steel-reinforced concrete was laid, compacted, levelled off and a float-finish applied, and work on the floor ended a week ahead of schedule. It dried enough to walk on over the weekend and a little topping-out ceremony was arranged. Everybody attended in good spirits and Stephen chipped in a crate of beer in addition to that supplied by the builders themselves.

The kennels interior was totally transformed and now a pleasure to walk around, as the men discussed the many problems that had been overcome and checked everything was working correctly. They tested the drains operation with buckets of water, and toasted the general success of the operation.

'Are you happy with it?' John asked Stephen as the builders chatted to kennel staff and watched muddy water flow freely along the concrete channels.

'I can hardly believe it John, it's a different place and I cannot thank you and your men enough.'

'So you've not minded us being around?'

'No, definitely not, it's been a pleasure watching you all work.'

'Well that's good because we're coming back next week.'

'Really, I thought you were finished?'

'We are but as there's a bit of time left over, we might as well whip the runs back up with the new partitions - it'll take us a quarter of the time it'd take you lot with your cable-ties and string.'

'That's great - we're running out of ties anyway!'

'Aye we'll sort that out for you; probably cut down some of the old cages and use them for barriers.'

'Right, good idea.'

'There's something else as well.'

'Is there?'

'Yes, I've noticed how hard you and your people work and how bad your facilities are - you've no canteen or even hot water so we've decided to bring Phase Two forward to make life a bit easier.'

'That'll be fantastic John but I thought you wanted to get out of here as fast as possible,' Stephen asked with a grin.

'I did,' John laughed. 'But I watch those kids grafting away every day and they deserve better conditions, and by the way, I've kind of got to like the atmosphere around here.'

'See John - I nearly said you'd get used to the noise and the smell!'

They both laughed and cracked a beer, and as soon as the runs were back in place and operational, John drafted in a squad of bricklayers to build the outer shell of the office block. He and Ryan cleaned up after them, completed the first fix ceiling, floor and partitions, then John stayed on his own to carry out the second and final fixes, and supervise the services installation.

Gary kept trying to drag him away but he always found something else that required his personal attention, and was there every day as the kennel staff enjoyed the luxury of new canteen facilities with hot running water! He made several suggestions to improve efficiency such as easy-access holders for rigid-leads, fold-up wall brackets to hold the weighing scales off the wet floor, and modifications to the purpose-made isolation pen for safely assessing incoming dogs. While John was working on this pen Stephen received a call from a contact in the Bristol area, asking if he could take in a terrified little mongrel from Romania.

'Romania?' he asked.

'Yes she's a harmless young bitch who's spent her whole life so far in a horrific kill-shelter.'

'Shit, really?'

'Yes, the poor little girl's totally petrified of everybody and everything, and we're told that she only survived the shelter this far because she spent all day every day - wedged between a wall and a packing crate, staring into the corner so she couldn't see or hear the horrors and mayhem going on all around her.'

'She'll be seriously traumatised.'

'She's a shivering wreck, Stephen. She was actually

born in the shelter so hasn't known anything else, and has never even been out in the open air.'

'Holy shit.'

'Neither her mother or siblings survived and we can't do anything with her - she's just too frightened to respond so if you can't help her – nobody can and she's finished.'

'Get her out of there as soon as you can and I'll meet you at your Sheffield office to collect her,' Stephen said, walking across and asking John if he could speed up completion of the isolation pen.

'Romania?' asked John in surprise when Stephen told him the story. 'Haven't we got enough strays in our own country to be going on with?'

'We have but she's just an animal in need to me - she doesn't know anything about countries and borders - she's spent her whole life in a corner at a kill-shelter, bless her.'

'Aye, suppose you're right, and if you're the only person who's willing and able to help her, then that's what you should do.'

The medium-sized, black & tan mongrel had to be sedated and crated to travel in the back of a van for 4 days, then transferred still in the crate to Stephen's truck, and at last to salvation at Shak. Until that day she had never been touched directly by a human hand. She arrived just as John was putting the final touches to her pen, was placed inside with a bed and blankets and he stood back to look at her. 'She's terrified,' he said to himself as much as to anyone else. 'A terrified little girl who's been to hell and back, but at least she's safe and sound now.'

'That posh new pen you've made must seem like paradise to her - her own little garden of Eden.'

'As long a she doesn't go chasing any forbidden fruit.'

'I don't want anything forbidden to her now, John.'

'No, so what kinda name are you going to give her?'

'I think we just have.'

'Have we?'

'Yeah, I'm gonna call her Eden.'

John must have told his wife all about her that evening, because Stephen got a call from Pauline saying, 'Thank goodness you took that poor, tortured little girl in Stephen. It's distressing to think what might have happened to her if you hadn't.'

Eden had completely closed down on life and was too afraid to interact with either people or other dogs. Bringing her out of her tightly shut, protective shell would take time and consistent effort and was not guaranteed to ever happen, but old hand Lennox, Stephen's big Akita-cross houseguest, was one of the first to say hello:

Thirty Seven

NEW HORIZONS

The work was over and had been a great success, as had the temporary transfer of 16 dogs to George's private kennels. Susan had managed extremely well and the quieter surroundings had a calming effect on the dogs. Being a true gentleman and sympathetic to Shak's aims, George didn't charge for the 6 week period and was so pleasant to deal with, that Stephen decided it would be a good idea to place any dogs which became eligible for re-homing, with him. Of course he didn't expect to carry on using kennel space for nothing, and retaining Susan's services would require some very good fortune as well.

Neil the businessman had made sufficient profit from his vending-machine operation to start semi-retirement, and subsequently began helping out at Shak by collecting and storing donated goods in his high-roofed, long-wheelbase van. He also moved dogs in crates and made urgent runs to the vet, and overall was a great help. He often delivered supplies to George's kennels, where he met Susan and was impressed by her managerial efficiency. Not long afterwards a suitable job came up elsewhere and she announced that regrettably, she'd have to leave Shak. During one of many chats over Friday evening beers in the Shoulder, Neil said to Stephen, 'Susan's doing a great job over there, she has the place running like clockwork and we shouldn't lose her if we can avoid it.'

'I know Neil but she's going to a paid job and nobody can blame her for that.'

'So why don't you pay her?'

'I'd love to but we just can't afford it.'

'What kind of money is she looking for?'

'Not sure but I can't even afford to pay her the minimum wage.'

'Think she'd stay for that?'

'She might; she definitely loves working with dogs.'

'She's good at it as well and I've been thinking - what if I pay her wages?'

'You'd do that?'

'I think so, it would definitely be good for Shak and my finances in the long-term, but I'd do it on a rolling, monthly basis to see how it all worked out.'

'So you'd be like an employment agency supplying her to us?'

'Something like that, what do you think?'

'I think it would be fantastic and we would all be very grateful.'

'Good, and while we're on the subject - you're seriously short of staff at the main kennels so why don't I finance two more people up there as well?'

'Honestly? I cannot tell you how much that would help us out and improve the dogs' lives, but I don't know how we could ever thank or repay you.'

'Don't worry about that - you just reorganise the workload and I'll make sure everything else is in place.'

Stephen told Rachel and his mother, who were both overjoyed knowing that doubling the staff would ease the mental and physical strain on all of them, and definitely make things better for the dogs who could have more time spent on them and get out for more exercise and fresh air.

Long term volunteer Richard was an obvious choice for employment and recruiting the second member of staff turned into 2 people, because Amy & Brad were both excellent workers, had been travelling all the way

246

from their home in Edinburgh to volunteer, and were a couple. Both displayed loyalty and leadership qualities, and jointly did most of the organising during their shifts.

Rich with Daisy

Things were definitely on an upward curve from the dark days they'd experienced around Christmas, and were going so well that Neil paid off the large vet bill and took on 2 additional, part-time workers: Sarah and Katherine as a new, upbeat mood spread amongst the staff.

One bright morning as Stephen manoeuvred his van around the Keel Row car park in Blyth, after checking out some reduced-price pet food at the market, he received a phone call from dog warden, Malcolm:

'Hello Stephen, I'm in a bit of a rush at the moment so to come straight to the point - can you take a Staffie with attitude?'

Stephen laughed. 'Good attitude or bad?'

'Depends on your point of view.'

'Can I collect him tomorrow because I've managed a day off now we have extra staff, and am over in Blyth?'

'It'll have to be today I'm afraid, I have a big meeting tomorrow which is likely to drag on all day, but I could drop him off this afternoon?'

'Okay, there are two staff members on duty so do that if you don't mind, Malcolm?'

He didn't mind too much and Stephen was able to make the most of his day off by catching up on supplies and their sources. He felt a little refreshed next morning as he entered the kennels and asked, 'So how's our new guest with the attitude then?'

Receiving a silent, blank stare from Melissa, he knew they had problems and asked, 'That bad?'

'Did you know about the collar and chain situation?'

'Er, no I don't think so, what's the problem?'

'Come and have a look,' she answered, leading the way to the isolation pen.

He looked through the bars from a yard away, grimaced and asked, 'Holy shit, how'd that happen?'

The dog's left foreleg was jammed through his collar as if wearing it as a sash, and the stretched leather bit deeply into his armpit and neck, around which also hung a thick chain.

'No idea, we thought you might know?'

Stephen took a step forward and the tortured dog turned into a snapping, snarling monster. He was obviously in pain and so angry about what had happened to him, that he gave clear warning of the consequences to anybody who approached.

'He's obviously a bit stressed,' Stephen said. 'So we'll leave him to calm down and figure out a plan to free him. Did Malcolm tell you much?'

'He told us what he knew.'

'Which is?'

'He was abandoned outside the visitor centre at Once Brewed.'

'At where?'

'That's what *I* said.'

'It's where the Pennine Way runs alongside the Roman Wall, just this side of Haltwhistle,' offered David, dumping soiled bedding on a pile by the main door.

'I learn something new every day working here. So has he been like this since he arrived?'

'Yes, you should have seen him when he first got here, we thought he was gonna have Malcolm's hand off!'

'Mm, okay well I'm going to have a think about the best way of sorting him out, and the first thing to do will be to get those straps and chains off him. Has he got a name?'

'Not that we know of.'

'Well I think we should call him Ged which I'm told is Gaelic for brave, because he definitely must be to put up with the pain he's obviously in.'

A few weeks previously Stephen received an email from a lady called Emma, who worked for the BBC. She'd heard about Shak, was researching for a programme about the increasing problem of stray dogs, and wondered if he'd be interested in taking part.

It sounds like a pretty good idea, he thought after hearing that they wanted to feature a dog which was a difficult case - and then show viewers what can be done in the right circumstances.

Stephen knew he now had the perfect candidate for what the BBC wanted - if only he could manage to show some progress with the dog. He thought long and hard and then called Emma on the number she'd left him. She was definitely interested, but he still had to free the Staffie and couldn't wait around for the BBC to show up. If he could use the situation as visual evidence though, that no dog is ever totally lost then he had to do that as well, by showing some initial aggression followed by the results of Shak's work. He had to be certain that the difference was plain for all to see, but the dog must not be allowed to suffer in the meantime so the question was exactly how to do that?

They fed and watered the dog and pushed plenty of bedding into his cage to make him as comfortable as possible for the night, and next morning Stephen went to work early. He told David and Melissa the BBC might be on their way and asked if they were willing to participate. Both agreed so he rooted around in the tool shed until he found an old pole-hook, shaped like a shepherds' crook, which had been lying around since before Shak took over the kennels. He asked David to grab a rigid-leash from the new rack, plus a pair of bolt-cutters donated by the builders and led the way towards the isolation pen.

Poking the pole slowly through the bars as Melissa filmed the operation on her smart-phone, he edged it towards the tormented Staffie as it stood motionless, watching every move with a wary eye. As the hook touched the chain around its neck the dog erupted into frenzied barking, lunging and twisting in somersaults to avoid what it assumed was another painful attack. Fearing the over-stressed animal might seriously injure itself, particularly with its left foreleg still caught up in the strap around its neck, Stephen pulled the pole away.

'Have to put a bit more thought into that,' he said to David and Mel who stood silently watching with doubtful expressions.

He backed off so the dog could settle, propped the pole against the canteen wall, tripped over the step and stumbled inside to sit down for a moment, wondering whether he should just call Emma to cancel her visit. He was nowhere near confident that he could free the Staffie from its bondage without sedation, and if he failed again it might be on everybody's television screens for all to see. He'd look like a failure and that perception would transfer directly to Shak, with devastating effects. So what should he do - bottle out and cancel, or man-up and do his best?

He got up and walked to the door, looking left to see David and Melissa still standing by the pen, equipment in hand awaiting further instruction. From behind the bars Ged stared straight out as if challenging him to try again, and fail. The scene was set and the BBC were coming to film the results, but was he up to the challenge? Did he have the courage to put himself, his reputation and his charity on the line for all to judge, or should he back out and live to fight another day?

He sat on the step thinking for a long time, until his deliberations were interrupted by the sound of heavy boots clumping across the concrete.

'We gonna try again then?' David asked.

Stephen turned back to the canteen as if in retreat. Melissa was about to say something but he picked up his pole, nodded at her and David and walked slowly to join them at the pen. As he approached, the troubled dog lowered its massive head and tensed as if to lunge. Painful memories of Troy's attack flashed through his mind and he froze for a few seconds, before slowly lifting the pole and showing it to the dog to avoid any sudden surprises. It sniffed the hook but kept looking at Stephen, who maintained eye contact as he passed it gently through the bars. The dog remained perfectly still and apparently calm as the hook glided towards him, until it touched the chain when once again he went berserk, grabbing the shaft between his powerful jaws and shaking it.

This time though, Stephen managed to keep the hook flat and steady, push it underneath the chain, turn it up and grasp the links as the dog pulled back. The bewildered animal twisted and turned and tried to break free, but Stephen pulled the pole gently towards him, moving the hook and chain up the dog's neck until it felt the push against its ears. Realising that Stephen was attempting to free it from its fetters, it stopped moving and stood still with head slightly lowered.

Stephen eased the chain gently forward until it slipped over the dog's head and fell to the ground. The Staffie grunted and looked down at the discarded metal, and then at Stephen. It remained still though nervous as he removed the pole in exchange for the rigid-leash which David handed him. He pushed it slowly forward, dropped the slip-noose over Ged's head and gently tightened it.

David opened the gate and Stephen manoeuvred Ged out, keeping him at a metre's distance while David curled the pole-hook around the collar. Mel then took hold of the leash and Stephen carefully cut through the hardened leather with the bolt-crops. Ged relaxed immediately and sat on his haunches, and for the first time Stephen knew they could really help him.

Stephen with Ged and Eden

The BBC crew came out 3 times in all to film, and then follow up on the story after Stephen had time to work with the dog. By then Ged was wearing a new soft collar which fit him correctly, and was walking calmly on a loose lead. Chris Jackson did a short interview with Stephen as well as with Emily at Moorview Vets, to compare views on the subject.

'It was a combined effort,' Stephen said as the team watched the Inside Out programme on 16 October 2017. 'We all worked together to make it possible and I couldn't do any of it without every one of you.'

'Well it certainly worked,' commented Joan. 'Ged's a different dog now as are all the others who come to us.'

'He is but to be honest, his quiet, calm nature was always there inside him, just waiting to be let out again. We can stroke and play with him now and he's been to stay at my house, where he got along with everybody including the other eight canine guests up there.'

'Well let's hope we can all stay together and the public continues its support so Shak can carry on doing what it does.'

'I was so proud of the little fella that day,' he said to Rachel as he topped up their celebratory drinks. 'And I'm proud of you and all the others who've ever given one minute of their time to help us.'

'Here's hoping they continue to do so,' she replied, clinking her glass of red against his. 'Because we desperately need every one of them and every penny we receive if we're going to carry on.'

'And here's to the first dog who inspired me to make the past twelve years a success - the dog who still brings a tear to my eye even now when I think of him, and who the charity is actually named after - beloved Shak.'

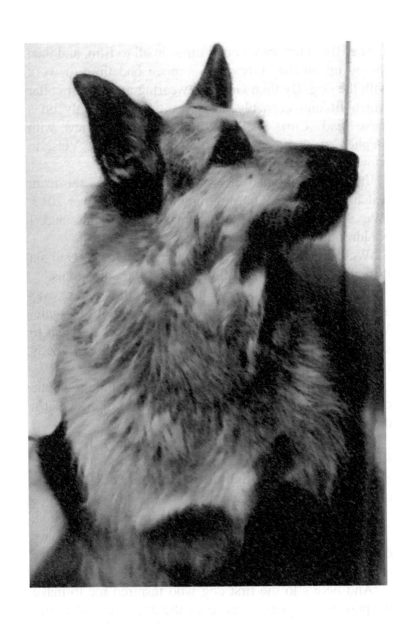

SHAK (*Registered Charity number: 1125159*) can only continue its unique work with the help of donations from the public. Help to save abused, neglected and condemned dogs from death row by visiting:
www.shak.org.uk

or emailing:
shak@shak.org.uk

or posting to:
SHAK,
Greenwell Road,
Alnwick,
Northumberland NE66 1HB.

(*Please note that no dogs are kept at these premises*).

'He is your friend, your partner, your defender, your dog.
You are his life, his love, his leader.
He will be yours, faithful and true, to the last beat of his
heart.
You owe it to him to be worthy of such devotion.'
(Anonymous)

Let them live and run free